Praise for

"Instead of an idealized (unrealistic) depiction of 'supermom,' with disarming honesty Julia Roller describes both the difficulties and surprising growth that can be found in the many beauties and struggles of motherhood. And rather than a prescription of more tasks to put on your spiritual to-do list, *Mom Seeks God* depicts the spiritual disciplines as freeing invitations—opportunities to peel back the 'mom' label and be the real you with God. In this courageously vulnerable book, Roller depicts for us a spiritual richness mined through the deep, hard soul-work of parenting."
—Kelli B. Trujillo, author of *The Busy Mom's Guide to Spiritual Survival* and the Flourishing Faith devotional series

"My friend Julia Roller has written a wonderful book for moms who long to freshly connect with God. She explores spiritual disciplines in a beautifully honest, practical, and humorous way. Bravo, Julia! What a wonderful resource for all of us."
—Rebecca St. James, singer, author, actress, and new mom

"Any parent who has ever struggled with feelings of inadequacy will appreciate Julia Roller's companionable memoir of her experiences with twelve—make that ten—spiritual practices. Written for readers who feel guilt at the very word prayer and terror at the idea of an all-out fast, this book offers a friendly introduction to spiritual practice."
—Jana Riess, author of *Flunking Sainthood* and *The Twible*

"I love how Julia says what I didn't have words for at the time I had small children. Once I got past the thought that I should have a deeper desire for God, and turned myself in to the notion that, while I didn't always want to spend time with God, I desperately needed him, that's when God became real to me as a mom. Julia gives us ancient wisdom boiled down into doable steps so that we can experience our beautiful God in the midst of our messy lives."
—Kathi Lipp, author of *The Husband Project* and *21 Ways to Connect with Your Kids*

"Julia Roller has given a tremendous gift to new parents, especially moms, with *Mom Seeks God*. In her quest to dive deep into spiritual disciplines, Julia provides practical practices to connect with God, growing

one's faith. The tips from other moms sprinkled throughout add to the breadth of the book and the necessity of spiritual growth while on the journey of parenthood."
—Becky Danielson, M.Ed., cofounder of 1 Corinthians 13 Parenting, coauthor of *Empowered Parents*

"No one ever tells you that motherhood is some of the most amazing spiritual training ground around. Which is why I'm thrilled Julia Roller does it in *Mom Seeks God*! New moms and veteran moms alike will love and learn from what Roller has to say about discovering God and practicing the disciplines right in the midst of motherhood."
—Caryn Rivadeneira, author of *Known and Loved*

"How appropriate that it was in the midst of feeling chaotic and overwhelmed that I sat down to read Julia's book on practicing the disciplines of a Christian walk. I was immediately renewed in my soul and the rest of the busy-ness seemed to shift into perspective. Julia shares her journey, complete with the successes and the struggles. She reminds us to get up, each day, and try again. There is no tomorrow or yesterday, only today. Spend some time today with the Lord."
—Crystal Lutton, author of *Biblical Parenting* and *Grace-Based Living*

"Becoming a mom rocked me to my core—where I once was a pulled together, semi-organized, semi-productive member of society, my life suddenly melted into chaos all fueled by one tiny little boy. It was chaotic, yes, but it was also a time of intense longing for God. I remember feeling an almost desperate urge to draw closer to God so that I could be the woman that he created me to be and the mom that my son needed. Julia Roller's book *Mom Seeks God* meets seeking moms like me where they are, telling them how to pray, fellowship, serve, and love in a way that draws us closer to the only One we need."
—Erin MacPherson, author of The Christian Mama's Guide series

"It is no secret that having a child profoundly changes our spiritual lives. We are never the same. Julia's honest, forthright, and beautifully described journey of practically pursuing the with-God life in the midst of motherhood is an encouragement to me as a fellow mom and follower of Jesus. I know it will be an encouragement to you as well."
—Rachel Quan, Executive Director, *Renovaré*

MOM SEEKS GOD

FINDING GRACE
IN THE CHAOS

Julia Roller

Abingdon Press
Nashville

MOM SEEKS GOD
FINDING GRACE IN THE CHAOS

Copyright © 2014 by Julia Roller

Library of Congress Cataloging-in-Publication Data has been requested.

ISBN 978-1-4267-7102-6

Scripture quotations unless noted otherwise are from the Common English Bible. Copyright © 2011 by the Common English Bible. All rights reserved. Used by permission. www.CommonEnglishBible.com.

Scripture quotations noted NRSV are taken from the *New Revised Standard Version of the Bible,* copyright 1989, Division of Christian Education of the National Council of the Churches of Christ in the United States of America. Used by permission. All rights reserved.

14 15 16 17 18 19 20 21 22—10 9 8 7 6 5 4 3 2 1
MANUFACTURED IN THE UNITED STATES OF AMERICA

To Ben and Luke,
my greatest gifts,
and to Ryan,
my partner in the journey

CONTENTS

CONTENTS

FOREWORD

The daring aim of the Christian spiritual disciplines is to produce in us a certain kind of person: a person who increasingly is penetrated through and through by love and joy and peace and patience and kindness and goodness and faithfulness and gentleness and self-control. Even more, the spiritual disciplines seek to bring us into a certain kind of life: a "with-God" kind of life.

Today the crying need is to learn exactly how this growing formation of the human personality and this "with-God" kind of life actually work smack-dab in the midst of our individualized, real-life experiences. This is precisely what Julia Roller does for us in the context of being a new mom. Mothering, in and of itself, is a colossal, multifaceted undertaking. Add to that sincere, well-meaning efforts to "practice the presence of God," and a new mom can quickly set herself up for disaster. As Julia confesses, "I was no longer practicing the presence [of God] because I was too busy attempting to practice two other things: maternal perfection and its companion, inadequacy."

Julia gets up close and personal as she describes for us the messiness and unpredictability of being a new mom to Ben, a rambunctious little guy, with another child coming soon. And all of this right in the middle of a full-time career as a writer and editor.

One striking and wholly attractive feature of *Mom Seeks God* is Julia's willingness to share with us the failures just as fully as the successes in her efforts to discover a life with God in the chaos of sleepless nights and smelly diapers. She describes, for example, how she kept banging up "against the craggy wall of my own sinfulness" and how "the problem for me was my old friend, the will."

Julia shares with us her learning and her growing as well. But the learning and the growing do not come by way of mastery or success. "You don't get to conquer parenting," she observes. Exactly. And we don't conquer the spiritual life either. Indeed, how can we conquer a reality in which the main point is to be conquered? No, in the spiritual life, as in parenting, we come as learners. And believe me, we shall forever be learners. That is how we grow in this life.

Of course, as a new mom Julia experiences a multitude of heart-bursting, joy-filled moments: Ben's first smile, his giggle, his tiny hand grasping Mommy's finger. With great tenderness she invites us into those "moments where the happiness just smacks you in the face and you feel a little dizzy with the force of it all." I'm glad Julia does this, for joy and delight are also key ingredients in the practice of the spiritual disciplines. Think of Saint Francis, that joyful troubadour of the Lord, tramping throughout the countryside inebriated with the love of God. The life that is pleasing to God does not come by gritting our teeth but by falling in love. And what is true with God is also true with our children.

Through her yearlong experience of discovering a "with-God" life through her mothering, Julia learned to let go of obsessive organizing and multitasking. "It's okay," she observes, "even preferable, to have long periods of unscheduled time." So it is. In our ongoing and deepening relationship with our children . . . and with God . . . we do well to allow for the lavish and easy wasting of time together.

This is a book for mothers, to be sure. But it is just as much a book for fathers. Indeed, it contains ample life lessons for parents-to-be and for parents-who-have-been. The stories charm us. The lessons instruct us. The insights guide us. *Tolle lege*, take and read.

—Richard J. Foster

INTRODUCTION: THE SPIRITUAL CRISIS OF MOTHERHOOD

I lay back on the hospital bed, sweaty and exhausted and still a little surprised that childbirth had not actually killed me. Then the nurse handed me a tiny, screaming bundle wrapped in a white blanket and sporting a pink-and-blue cap too big for his tiny head. His eyes were bright red from the routine antibiotic ointment the nurse had just applied, and his skin looked whiter than pale in comparison, like a tiny Voldemort. He was the most gorgeous thing I'd ever seen. I even loved his screams, knowing a wailing newborn was likely a healthy newborn. He finally calmed and pursed his lips, his eyes seeming to fix on mine. I wondered if he knew who I was.

"I'm your mommy," I told him, and as I said the words, I realized they were true. I was this baby's mommy, and that had changed everything.

An hour later, as an orderly wheeled the two of us down the hall to the elevator, I still couldn't take my eyes off my new baby. Benjamin. I felt literally swollen with pride that this little creature was mine, so much so that if someone bumped me, little sparks of satisfaction might come shooting out. I was sure everyone around me, including that poor orderly working the night shift and pushing sweaty, disheveled me around was just as mesmerized by this tiny bundle. How could they not be?

So this was what it felt like, to fall in love in an instant.

I knew Ben's birth would change my life. That my schedule, my abs, my sleep requirements were never going to be the same.

But what I did not know was how profoundly his birth would change my spiritual life. The way I felt about this tiny baby offered a glimpse into the depths of God's love for us. That fierce, protective love I felt after giving birth only grew stronger as I got to know little Ben. I couldn't get enough of the way his lips pursed as he slept. I thought I might pass out from joy the first time he smiled at me. As he grew, I realized that watching him enjoy himself was light-years more fun and rewarding than actually enjoying something on my own, certainly the most profound insight I've ever had into why God might have created us.

Yet motherhood also laid bare my weaknesses and selfishness in a way nothing else ever had. Just a few weeks after he was born, we realized he was failing to gain weight, despite my breastfeeding him around the clock. *I* had failed to adequately sustain the life entrusted to me. The combination of this abiding sense of failure, the sleeplessness and exhaustion exacerbated by a draconian feeding and pumping schedule, and a medication I was prescribed to increase my breast milk led me into a brief but dark depression. All I could think was, *Only eighteen more years of this, and I'll be free.* Then I would feel guilty and ashamed. How thin was my faith that the minute things got tough, I went completely to pieces? It took this radical reorientation of my life, this compulsory focus on another person, for me to realize how focused I had always been on myself. I loved this tiny baby, yet I desperately wanted life to go back to the way it had been before.

I was not alone in this feeling. In a recent study, 92 percent of moms agreed that motherhood was the hardest job they'd ever attempted.

Things did get better, thankfully, and as my son and I learned and grew together through his first two years, I was able to view motherhood as the privilege it was, something to enjoy rather than something to endure. Yet I still banged up against the craggy wall of my own sinfulness. When Ben grew into a toddler and lost his temper, I often lost my own temper right back. I sometimes picked him up more roughly than I should have. I muttered things under my breath I never thought I'd say. Again and again, I was confronted by the limits of my patience, and the limitlessness of my selfishness.

I needed God; I needed forgiveness, but the ways I had been accustomed to meeting God no longer seemed to fit into my life. I was too tired to pray at night or, after multiple nighttime feedings, to get up any earlier in the morning. How could I find time to study the Bible when I still hadn't figured out how to go to the bathroom by myself?

It wasn't that I never prayed, but all I was managing anymore was a reactive kind of prayer. *I can't believe I just had to lock myself in the bathroom to calm down. Again. I'm sorry, God. Why can't I be more patient?* And even those kinds of prayers were becoming less frequent. You can get out of the habit of prayer pretty easily, I found.

The kind of prayer I'd always felt most connected to was the "practicing the presence" method of Brother Lawrence, a French monk from the seventeenth century. In *The Practice of the Presence of God*, Brother Lawrence describes how he grew disillusioned with set times of prayer and gradually learned to be in constant communication with

God, even, and perhaps especially, amid the noise of the monastery kitchen where he worked. While I'd never come close to Brother Lawrence's constant communication, I'd always loved this idea of talking to God during the busyness of daily life as well as in the quiet and silence. I often had my best times of prayer when I was walking or writing or doing things around the house.

It seemed this concept would be especially applicable to motherhood, but that was not immediately the case for me. This seemed in part because of the new lack of quiet in my house. Before, I might have been walking or showering or making the bed while I was praying, but it was still quiet if I wanted it to be. Suddenly I had a constant tiny companion—a very cute but very noisy and often demanding companion. Shortly after Ben was born, my mother sent me an article about how children's verbal success later in life could be traced back to the number of words they heard each day as infants. From that point on I felt obligated to keep up a running commentary of everything I was doing for my audience of one. "Mommy is driving us to class. Mommy is late again. Mommy is frustrated by the pedestrians who cross the street everywhere *but* the crosswalk. Remind Mommy not to talk to anyone at class because she forgot to brush her teeth. Again." It felt awfully weird to be describing everything to a baby who didn't do much more than cry, sleep, and eat. But I was nothing if not dutiful about motherhood, and, given my early failure to properly feed him, I was determined to get everything else right. So there I was, announcing to Ben that I was changing his diaper. And that we were walking down the street, and that the grass was green, and the sidewalk was gray. And that Mommy was losing her mind.

You may wonder why I didn't just pray aloud. One reason was that I had never really made a practice of praying aloud and so it felt awkward, but the main reason is harder to admit—that I didn't really feel like it. I was no longer practicing the presence because I was too busy attempting to practice maternal perfection and its companion, inadequacy. I knew that without quiet time with God, I wasn't managing to talk to God when it was noisy. But I had to admit that even when I did find quiet, I wasn't spending it with God. Instead, I worried about doing everything right or complained to myself.

I'd always loved the image of Brother Lawrence joyfully seeking and finding God among the pots and the pans, and in my new schedule, much of my precious quiet time, my son's naps, was also spent among the pots and the pans. I spent all morning, it seemed, looking forward to Ben's half-hour nap. But when I did get him down, a manic switch flipped on in my brain. All those things I thought I could only do when I didn't need to supervise or entertain him stacked up in my mind, and I would dash madly around the apartment doing a little bit each of twenty-five different tasks, completing none. A constant naptime priority was the dishes that continually piled up on the counter and in the sink of our tiny galley-style kitchen. As I gazed out the window at the stucco homes and terra-cotta roofs of the sunny, beautiful Southern California community where we lived, hands deep in soapy water, I found myself filled not with Brother Lawrence's joy and peace, but with a low-level but near-constant sense of resentment. That my apartment was too small and didn't have a dishwasher. That Ben's naps weren't long enough even to finish washing the never-ending pile of dishes and bottles and breastfeeding/pumping accessories. That my husband worked too much and didn't do enough around the house. And on and on.

Much of my frustration stemmed from the lack of control I felt. I didn't seem to be able to get anything done. No longer was I the master of my own schedule. As anyone who has had a child knows, the ability to do what you want when you want is the first thing to go. Babies blow out their diapers, they fall asleep, they scream, they get sick, and all at the most inconvenient times. Of course, they also giggle contagiously, say "Mama" in the most adorable little voices, and react to the sight of you with such pure, open-mouthed joy that it brings tears to your eyes, all on their own schedule. I was still struggling to embrace all this unpredictability.

I had to figure out some ways to connect with God in my new life. Because it wasn't just about me anymore. There were little eyes watching me and all that I did, and I had to figure out how to guide them.

The Plan

For many years now, I'd been writing books about spiritual formation and spiritual disciplines. I'd first been introduced to these concepts in Richard J. Foster's remarkable book *Celebration of Discipline*. The ideas expressed there, and in other Renovaré books such as Dallas Willard's *The Great Omission*, were life-changing for me. The bedrock assumption of these books is that that once we become Christians, we are not "done." As important as it is to make a decision to invite Jesus in, and however important the implications of this invitation are for our eternal salvation, that isn't the end of the matter. It is only the beginning of a lifelong process of discipleship, of learning and growing to become ever more like Jesus. And God has afforded us, and Jesus has demonstrated for us, many different practices to help us along in this process of discipleship. Foster calls these tools spiritual disciplines, and they involve everything from prayer to fasting to celebration. Silence, solitude, and study are in there too.

Foster and other writers are very anxious to make it clear that the spiritual disciplines have nothing to do with our salvation, and that they have no worth in and of themselves. They are simply practices that we can engage in, practices that Jesus both taught and demonstrated, that help us become more like Jesus, and therefore, so much better equipped to help God with his work of the Kingdom.

I hadn't even realized, until after I'd read these ideas, how frustrated I'd felt with the way that I, a committed Christian, kept failing to live up to my ideals of what a Christian should be. As a hobby musician, I was especially attracted to Foster's analogy of how a beginning piano player must start slowly with simple songs, scales, and the like in order to one day play one of Chopin's études. How many times had I thought, unconsciously or not, that because I was a Christian I should just automatically exhibit all the fruit of the Spirit? Or wondered why, after being a Christian all my life, I still felt like such a beginner. What a beautiful and helpful corrective, this explanation of spiritual formation, and my own realization that it was okay to be just at the starting point, and that there were practices I could engage in to help myself along the road to Christlikeness. These practices helped me immensely when I had been able to engage in them, so it was doubly frustrating to feel cut off from them with the life changes accompanying new motherhood.

I became even more motivated to bring the spiritual disciplines back into my life when I was asked to write a devotional called *A Year with God* that would lead readers through the key biblical passages about eighteen different spiritual disciplines, such as prayer, silence, solitude, meditation, fasting, simplicity, and so on. As I embarked on this project, I found myself continually writing phrases like "In your daily prayer time . . . ," and I was again uncomfortably reminded of the fact that I didn't have a consistent daily time of prayer. Or even weekly prayer. Or, really, even monthly prayer.

I decided that as I studied what the Bible had to say about these key ways of meeting God, I would do my best to practice one discipline per month, to embark upon my own year with God. I suspected that reintroducing these disciplines into my life was largely a matter of priorities, and that if I started to value prayer, Bible study, and other Christian practices as highly as I did my writing and editing work and my gym time, to name just a few, then I would surely be able to figure out a place for them.

This book describes my resulting attempts to practice the spiritual disciplines in the midst of my life as a mother, wife, and writer. The process is ongoing, of course, but this book covers a yearlong effort. I planned to focus on twelve disciplines, one every month. It all went along okay for a while, with some disciplines feeling a lot easier to attempt than others. But then a big surprise came along in late summer, and, as surprises of this particular nature do, it managed to pretty much knock every other priority in my life off the list. So, rather than twelve disciplines, it became ten, and believe me when I tell you I mastered none. Yet, thankfully, mastery is not required. My mistakes and my disorganization—even my despair over feeling like a failure—were all part of the story of my learning to pay attention to God in my life. Spiritual practices aren't like tasks on your to-do lists; you don't get to check them off at the end of each day (although, wouldn't that be nice?). Instead, you just hold on to your intention and dive in, occasionally pausing to note what God has shown you so far. As we all know, life is unpredictable and messy. (Just look at, well, *any* page of the Bible.) Yet God still gets through to us, sometimes right in the middle of the chaos.

I believe God reached me powerfully through my year of seeking to know God better through these spiritual practices, despite my failings and inconsistencies. And not only am I immensely grateful for that, but I have also come to be more and more grateful for that emotional experience of coming face-to-face with my own weakness. As Christians such as C. S. Lewis and Thomas R. Kelly learned long before me, it is a gift to be able to see ourselves (and others) so clearly. According to Lewis and Kelly, the further along we are in our spiritual journeys, the more we see our own evil sides and just how terrible they really are. And if we can't see ourselves as we truly are, we cannot make progress.

Thank you for being willing to join me on my journey. I have also included in each chapter some of my friends' stories about how they have experienced and continue to experience God through these spiritual practices. I hope the ideas here will help you connect with God in new and deeper ways.

1

PRAYER: MAKING GOD A HABIT

January

*Praying with frequency gives us the readiness to pray again
as needed from moment to moment. The more we pray, the more we
think to pray, and as we see the results of prayer—
the responses of our Father to our requests—our confidence
in God's power spills over into other areas of our life.*
—Dallas Willard, *The Spirit of the Disciplines*

Prayer. Just the word made me feel slightly guilty.

There isn't much more basic to your relationship with God than prayer. Maybe that's why I always felt as though I didn't pray enough or in the right way. I had this idea that to be a true Christian, you were supposed to spend an hour or so each morning in silent prayer. There is biblical support for praying in the morning, and I'm sure it is indeed a very good thing to do, but it's not something I had ever managed, even pre-motherhood.

As a lifelong night owl, in the past I'd found bedtime to be a good time for prayer and reflection, but the impressive new heights of tired I'd reached since becoming a mom meant that my evening prayers now usually sounded like this: "Dear God, sorry that I was so impatient—[*snore*] . . ."

So when I resolved to bring spiritual disciplines more intentionally into my life, I knew I wanted to start with prayer. But how to begin?

So Many Prayers

In Richard J. Foster's book *Prayer*, he describes a dizzying twenty-one different kinds of prayer. Trying all twenty-one seemed a bit much for my month-long effort, like eating at a prayer buffet—a little bit of everything and not tasting or appreciating much of anything as a result. I decided I could manage a serious effort to practice three different kinds of prayer in turn: contemplative prayer, praying the Examen, and petitionary prayer.

First on my list: contemplative prayer. Contemplative prayer is, simply put, listening to God. In a place of quiet, you lift your mind to God and, instead of letting loose with a flood of thanks or wonder or petition, you let God show or teach you what God will. It is sometimes referred to as God-led therapy. Perhaps the most eloquent description of contemplative prayer is found in *The Cloud of Unknowing*, a book written by an anonymous author, probably an English monk, sometime in the fourteenth century: "Lift up your heart to God with a gentle stirring of love. Focus on him alone. Want him, and not anything he's made. Think on nothing but him. Don't let anything else run through your mind and will."

Solitude and silence are, if not mandatory prerequisites, certainly helpful conditions for practicing contemplative prayer. You can see why contemplative prayer appealed to a stressed-out mom who felt that she never got to be alone. It sounded very peaceful; it sounded a lot like what I was missing, in fact. So I planned to begin practicing contemplative prayer on January 1. Starting a new year with a renewed commitment to the spiritual disciplines may have been annoyingly New Year's resolution-y, but it also helped to add a bit of gravitas to the whole thing. As a practiced procrastinator, I knew if I didn't have a firm date, I'd put it off until Ben went to college.

Are You There, God? It's Me, Julia

Foster writes in *Prayer* that we don't have to pray all the time, that just a few minutes in God's presence can be refreshing and wonderful enough for those who are unused to it. It is probably a good indicator of the confidence I had in my contemplative ability that I took him at his word and decided to set an initial goal of only five minutes. To help me out, my husband, Ryan, took Ben with him on an errand so I could have a rare moment of peace and quiet in the house. Although I knew I should get started right away, I found myself delaying. First it seemed imperative that I listen to the Indigo Girls and Bono singing "Kid Fears" on iTunes. Then I had to figure out where to sit. The floor was too cold so I got up and fetched a blanket. Then, once I was wrapped in the blanket, I worried I would fall asleep, which, since Ben had yet to sleep through the night, was a real possibility anytime I was seated. I had literally fallen asleep while reading him a Thomas the Tank Engine story. When I finally settled into my office chair and closed my eyes, I tried to make my mind a blank screen for God to put an image or word or memory on, a technique I had read about.

I repeated the word "Jesus" a few times. It was quiet; all I heard was traffic and the occasional airplane. I enjoyed the silence but found myself a little tense, expecting that at any moment Ryan and Ben would walk in and shatter it. I also had to fight the urge to write down everything I was thinking or craft it into acceptable prose in my head. My thoughts jumped from an upcoming writing deadline to wondering whether or not I might be pregnant again. I thought about an episode I'd just watched of the TV show *House*, the plotline of which got me thinking about my public identity as a Christian. Then I wondered if thinking about TV shows was a sign that I should return to repeating "Jesus." The trouble was that I had no idea what thoughts were distractions and which might be guided thoughts from God.

I opened my eyes, thinking I had probably been sitting there much longer than my allotted five minutes. Nope. Two minutes. As I stared at the computer clock in disbelief, I heard Ryan and Ben return home.

The next day, I tried again, aiming for a whopping ten minutes this time. Ryan offered to time it for me so I wouldn't peek at the clock or worry about whether I'd gone too long or not long enough. In a letter to one of her many students, early twentieth-century writer Evelyn Underhill gives some practical advice for contemplative prayer, which I was trying my best to follow:

1. Put yourself into some position so easy and natural to you that you don't notice your body: and shut your eyes.

Clearly, even this first step didn't come easily for me. I had spent more time deciding where and how to sit yesterday than I'd actually spent praying. This time I went straight for my office chair, but again I found myself shifting and changing positions several times. I was worse than my dog, nudging and circling her bed before she settled down. Finally, I settled into a cross-legged position, what my son would call *crisscross applesauce*.

2. Represent to your mind, some phrase, truth, dogma, event—e.g., a phrase of the Paternoster or Anima Christi, *the Passion, the Nativity are the sort of things I use. Something that occurs naturally. Now, don't think about it, but keep it before you, turning it over as it were, as you might finger some precious possession.*

I wasn't quite as theologically sophisticated as Evelyn Underhill; I wasn't even 100 percent sure what she meant by *"Anima Christi."* But using nothing more complicated than "Jesus" seemed to work for me. I loved this idea of keeping his name before me as I might a precious possession, so I started by repeating his name aloud.

3. Deliberately, and by an act of will, shut yourself off from your senses. Don't attend to touch or hearing: till the external world seems unreal and far away. Still holding on to your idea, turn your attention inwards . . . and allow yourself to sink, as it were, downwards and downwards, into the profound silence and peace which is the essence of the meditative state. More you cannot do for yourself: if you get further, you will do so automatically as a consequence of the above practice. It is the "shutting off the senses" and what Boehme calls the "stopping [of] the wheel of the imagination and ceasing from self-thinking" that is hard at first.

I tried to sink inward and downward as she instructed and found that it came a little more easily. Already I felt more comfortable with letting thoughts come to me and then letting go of them when I felt ready, repeating "Jesus" when I thought I needed to return to center. I found myself thinking about my writing. I had been working for years on a fiction project, but all my paid work had been in nonfiction. I felt nudged toward the conclusion that this success in non-fiction writing was because that was where God wanted me to be, at least for now. When Ryan came in and told me that the ten minutes were up, I was surprised. I had been enjoying myself, not feeling restless at all.

And so it went with my contemplative prayer practice. Some days I never managed to get to it at all. Other days I found it incredibly difficult to sit still and even harder to still my brain, which insisted on running through my list of things to do. I realized that as much as I thought I wanted to pray more, I was having a hard time convincing myself to prioritize it over everything else that I had to do—clean the house, pay bills, do dishes, meet my writing deadlines. When I finally managed to take the time and relax in prayer, I often found myself thinking of the strangest things, like Mary's song from *Jesus Christ Superstar*, "I Don't Know How to Love Him." I had heard that dreams were the brain's way of taking out the trash. Was this also true of contemplative prayer?

I still struggled with the question of whether I was hearing God's voice or just my own. There were no easy answers to this question. Dallas Willard explains that it is experience that helps us discern when it is "just me" or when it is God's voice. The only solution, it seemed, was to spend more time listening.

What Works for Me

Andrea, literary agent and mother of two

I've been reading John Baillie's *A Diary of Private Prayer*, which includes morning and evening prayers that help me begin and end each day alert to God's presence. Of course, we're never absent from God, but with so many demands on my time, it can be a challenge to stay aware. Setting aside even a few moments for prayer and silence has helped me develop a more holistic stance toward life, where I know that I'm connected to God even in the mundane and busy parts of my day.

I soon discovered a few ways to ease more naturally into contemplative prayer. It helped when I set a timer or when someone else timed it for me. Otherwise, I engaged more in clock-watching than listening. And it worked better when I didn't try it toward the end of naptime, because otherwise I spent every minute of prayer bracing for a wail to break my concentration. Practice and consistency did make a difference. When I prayed every day, it seemed to come much more easily. Missing a day or two, on the other hand, seemed to make it that much harder to settle down to prayer the next time.

Then it all went wrong.

No Nap, No Prayer

It started innocently enough. Ben climbed out of the Pack 'n Play that had been his bed for the first two years of his life, so Ryan and I took him to IKEA for that toddler rite of passage: a big-boy bed. But now that he could get out of his bed anytime he wanted, he was no longer napping. At all. Those naps of his had been brief, but the short lulls they provided often felt like the time I needed to keep the house and myself together, not to mention my time for contemplative prayer. Without the naps, both Ben and I were increasingly short of temper. I found myself praying in the moment all the time, mostly for patience and for forgiveness when I lost it. What little contemplative prayer practice I'd managed had helped me get back in the routine of talking to God, but I still felt as though I had failed.

Since I no longer had naptime available for contemplative prayer, it occurred to me that I could try it at night. The time after Ben went to bed was my highly anticipated "free time," even though I often used it for very odd things. (If there are other people in the world who clean the burners at 2 a.m., I suspect they are also mothers of small children.) One night after I'd cleaned up the kitchen, I settled into my office chair and closed my eyes. To my surprise, I didn't find myself falling asleep, as I so often did when I tried to pray in bed. Maybe the key was as simple as praying while remaining upright.

It went well that night, yet I didn't feel I could consistently add a nightly contemplative prayer experience to my already packed post-Ben's-bedtime hours. For one thing, those hours were already getting crunched. Ben's bedtime was currently a very long game of "Go back to bed," with Ben hopping gleefully out of his new bed as soon as we left the room and poking his head into the hallway like a blond jackrabbit. And at some point I, too, needed to go to bed.

I had enjoyed spending quiet time with God. I still loved the idea of listening to God and the surprising thoughts that answered my call. I liked even more the revelation that it was something I could do at nighttime, which had always been my favorite set of hours. But I just couldn't seem to manage it right now, and I was starting to wonder if I had erred in choosing it in the first place. In *Prayer,* Foster writes that a lot of people avoid simple prayer (talking with God about all things, good and bad) in favor of more "sophisticated" types of prayer, and that this fallacy is often committed by those who don't really pray. Maybe I had started with contemplative prayer for the wrong reasons, maybe because it sounded more sophisticated, more intellectual.

Sometimes when something comes only with great difficulty, you are meant to keep pushing until you master it. Other times, it is a sign that you are climbing the wrong hill.

Praying the Examen

The next kind of prayer on my list was the prayer of Examen, first developed by Ignatius of Loyola, a sixteenth-century Christian leader. The central idea is of reflecting on, or examining, your day. Father Dennis Hamm, SJ, describes praying the Examen as "rummaging for God," an image I liked. There are many versions of the Examen, but the simplified one I decided to try involved two main parts. First, you review the day with the intention of finding Christ in it. In whom did you see Christ? Where in your day did you experience his nearness? Then, second, you try to open your heart to being examined and corrected by God. When in your day had you strayed from Christ? When were you far away from him? I still hadn't given up hope that I could pray at night, and one of the Examen's major selling points was that not only could I do it lying in bed at night, it was probably even better to do it then, so I could review the entire day. Somehow, the idea of praying in those last few minutes before sleep made it feel less like another thing to check off my to-do list, and I hoped that having an agenda would help keep me awake. Besides, I had never appreciated my bed as much as I had post-baby. I was so tired from still getting up with Ben once or twice most nights and early in the morning that when *my* bedtime came each night, I sank into bed with the most delicious feeling of relief and gratitude. I was primed for prayer.

That first night, I lay down and asked myself where I had seen Christ. Right away I thought of Ben's preschool teachers and how lovingly they had said good-bye to Ben when I picked him up. I thought of the kindness some bank employees had shown us that evening, when they'd stayed late to honor our requests. And I thought of both Ryan and Ben.

What was most surprising about reflecting on these ways I had seen Christ was how joyful it made me feel. Although in my own haphazard prayers, and in prayers before bedtimes and mealtimes with

Ben, I listed things for which to be thankful and to praise God, it felt different to focus instead on where Christ had been in our day. It made me think about the reality of Christ working in our world, and what was more hope-giving than dwelling on that?

As for thinking about where I had strayed from Christ, I came up with the usual: be more patient with Ben. I asked for forgiveness and resolved to do better.

I continued to pray the Examen every night before bed. I loved that I didn't have to time this kind of prayer. Often I could pray it very quickly and still feel as though I had spent quality time with God. Other times I spent quite a while thinking about specific ways in which I had strayed. I started to view each Examen as a strategy session with God, where we worked together to try to figure out how to handle things differently the next time. My failings were numerous, and again, most of them had to do with Ben, with losing patience or yelling or feeling frustrated with him. But reflecting on them in this way was not as painful as I had expected because the context of the Examen felt more about forgiveness and moving on than about shame and punishment. Instead, I actually felt grateful for God's showing me these failings and helping me think about how to do better. Those little strategy sessions seemed to help too. I found myself feeling more patient and calm during the day. And I continued to find it rewarding and joyful to think about the ways Christ entered my life, most often through Ben, my husband, my friends, and Ben's teachers, but also through nature, through books, and through brief interactions with people at the grocery store or on the street. It was surprising how much of God I found in these most mundane of events. Reflecting on God's presence at the end of each day seemed more realistic than ex-pecting myself to practice the awareness all day long. And at the same time, the nightly examining helped me become more aware of God's presence as I moved through the day.

Asking God

I had always planned to continue to add each new type of prayer to my existing practice, like building blocks in a prayer wall. How exactly this would work, I wasn't sure—whether I would do contemplative prayer on Tuesdays or Thursdays and the Examen Monday, Wednesday, and Friday or what. I hadn't planned exactly when I would switch from one type to the next either. With my typical seat-of-my-pants planning, I just figured I'd put them together in whatever way seemed to work best at the time.

I continued to pray the Examen at night, but I became aware of a feeling of restlessness, a sense of needing more. This restlessness seemed like a nudge from the Holy Spirit to face the last kind of prayer I wanted to try—the one I'd been putting off: petitionary prayer, or asking God.

I don't know why I had such complicated feelings about making requests of God. The Bible is full of examples of Jesus telling us that if we ask, we will receive. Even within the Lord's Prayer he instructed us to ask God for our daily bread, but the example that I always came back to was Jesus praying in the garden of Gethsemane just before he was arrested. I like the wording in Mark best, where Jesus says, "Abba, Father, for you all things are possible. Take this cup of suffering away from me. However—not what I want but what you want." This passage was one of my very favorites for what it said about Jesus, about God, and about the lengths they would go to out of their love for us. But what did it tell us about prayer? Jesus asks but doesn't ask. Instead, he acquiesces to God's will. And even though, as noted above, Jesus said we will receive whatever we ask for, we also read in James 4:3 about people who did not receive what they asked for because they asked with wrong motives.

So I concluded that we were to ask but also to be cautious that our requests were in line with God's will, and that caveat stressed me out—did God even care about a lot of the little things I fretted over? Agnes Sanford writes, "When we pray in accordance with the law of love, we are praying in accordance with the will of God." Helpful words but, like so many wise words about prayer, awfully vague. I had even more questions. Should I pray by lifting my concerns up in a general sense and asking God to guide me, or boldly ask for very specific things? Both?

I was finally helped by reading how Richard Foster went through the entire New Testament and noted each instance of Jesus praying or teaching about prayer. Foster realized that when Jesus prayed for other people, he always prayed with utter confidence that his request would be granted. It was only when Jesus prayed for himself, as in the garden of Gethsemane, that he added the caveat about God's will being done rather than Jesus' own. It is hard to overstate how helpful this teaching was for me. I grew much more confident in praying for other people, even in ways that had previously made me uncomfortable, from laying my hand on a pregnant friend and asking that her twins be delivered safely to praying that another close friend become pregnant. But, following Foster's insight, I still felt hesitant about asking for such things for myself, so I decided to focus my prayers on petitions for others.

Foster advises to start small, not with stage 4 cancer, for example, and not to expect big results at first. As I thought about where to start asking for others, I struggled to put aside my own overriding concern—how crunched I was for work time. I depended on the couple of hours

Ben was in preschool three days a week for writing time, but he'd woken up with yellow gunk streaming steadily from his nose, and I knew he'd have to miss at least two days of school. I felt anxiety threatening to overwhelm me as I started calculating how far back these missed hours would set me. I had never been able to work with Ben at home, unless he was asleep. He wanted and needed my attention, especially when he wasn't feeling well, of course, so I had to chalk those hours up to mommy time rather than work time. I felt powerless and frustrated, knowing that I'd have to stay up until the wee hours in order to catch up.

It was one of the most difficult things to get used to about motherhood, the way even a runny nose completely derailed my writing schedule. I felt incredibly lucky to be able to work from home because I could be with Ben almost all the time and still keep a job I loved. But juggling mommyhood and working at home sometimes blew up in my face. I'd plan out my writing time, and then it would disappear before my eyes like an evil conjuring trick. *Poof!*

Ben's illness, it seemed, was a perfect opportunity for petitionary prayer. But I had set the goal of praying for other people's needs rather than my own. Of course I wanted him to feel well because I loved him and hated to see him suffer, but mostly I wanted him to be better so I could meet my deadline . . . and I knew it.

Instead, that night I prayed that my constantly sleep-deprived husband would have a restful and refreshing night's sleep, knowing that he would have to get up at 5 a.m. the next day, Saturday, and first go to work and then teach a class at a local university where he was an adjunct professor. These Saturday classes were hard on him. Afterward, he routinely came home, turned on a soccer game, and fell asleep on the couch for a good part of the afternoon. I asked God for Ryan to feel rested and strong. It seemed like a good example of starting small and of praying for someone else's need.

This focus on praying for someone else, per Jesus' example, seemed especially important right then because I felt so panicky and overwhelmed about my own needs—that I wouldn't meet my deadline, that I wouldn't get the house looking halfway decent for my parents' and Ryan's parents' upcoming visits, that I wouldn't be able to manage this poor sick little guy. I hoped that praying for someone else would help me to stop feeling sorry for myself. And the prayer did seem successful. Ryan told me the class went very well, and the one who fell asleep on the couch that afternoon was me, not him!

But it didn't seem to prevent me from wallowing in my own problems. My next deadline was now only a week away, and writing time was not miraculously appearing. Something we enjoyed doing as a family was going to Ryan's rec league soccer games on Sunday nights and then out to dinner. I'd never missed a game before, but I was so far behind that I finally called a friend and asked him to sit with Ben at the game so I could stay home and work.

Feeling sad and frustrated over having to sacrifice family time, I nonetheless wrote until 2 a.m., and as I dragged my groggy self out of bed Monday morning, I thought again about the night before. I had focused so much on the fact that I had to miss the game that I'd nearly missed the fact that I was lucky enough to have a friend who could take Ben to the game so I could have writing time and Ben didn't have to miss out. Plus, Ben seemed well enough to go to school that day, and, truthfully, that made me feel better about everything. While he was there, I finished an entire section of the book. That meant I had only two more sections to go before my February 1 deadline, and I finally felt like it was within reach. Had God heard my anxiety even though I had been trying not to pray deliberately for my own needs? All I knew for sure was that I was grateful.

Bullying God

The next couple of days, however, Ben seemed sicker. His nose was running again, and he had a terrible cough. In the midst of his illness, I found myself turning to a prayer by Martin Luther titled "For Assurance of Being Heard":

> Lord God, heavenly Father, I ask for and need assurance that my petitions may be nothing less than yes and amen. Otherwise I will not pray or have intercession made for me. Not that I am righteous or worthy, for I know very well and confess that I am unworthy. With my great and many sins I have earned your eternal wrath and hell fire.
>
> But because you command and constrain me to pray in the name of your dear Son, our Lord Jesus Christ, I am still somewhat obedient. Not because of my own righteousness, but because of your infinite goodness, do I kneel or stand before you. I pray for what is upon my heart concerning those in need of your help. If you do not help them, O Lord, you will offend and dishonor your name. Surely you will save your reputation so that the world will not say you are an ungracious and a dreadful God. Preserve us from such misfortune.
>
> Remember, dear heavenly Father, how you have at all times supported and helped your people. I will not stop knocking but will continue crying aloud and pleading to the end of my life. Amen.

Was Martin Luther actually bullying God? Was that allowed? Was *this* what it meant to ask boldly? I would never have thought of addressing God that way, yet I couldn't help but notice that Luther matched his boldness with such humility. And that last line about continuing to cry aloud reminded me how much I've always loved (and been more than a little awed by) the idea that we as Christians have the privilege of helping God with his Kingdom work. Praying was one important way of doing so.

The next day Ben had to miss school again. We were practically out the door, both dressed and ready to go, when I looked at his still-streaming nose and thought, *I can't*. Then I burst into tears, not because I was missing work time, but because it was the day of the once-a-year Art Experience where parents were invited to attend with their children and spend all morning working on art projects together. I couldn't believe we had to miss it. It seemed as if this cold would never end.

We played for a while, read books, and then I settled him into his bed for a nap. (The one benefit of this cold was that it had brought back the naps.) I went into my office and came before God with my petitions again. First I thanked God for hearing my prayer for Ryan since I had noticed that he seemed to be more rested. I wondered if I was being presumptuous in assuming any perceived change was due to my prayer, but I chalked such thoughts up to my inner cynic. When in doubt, thank.

Now that Ben and I had already missed the special art class and he didn't have school for a few days, I felt more confident about praying for his cold, that I didn't have to worry so much about my motives. I tiptoed into his room and hovered awkwardly above him, listening to his congested breathing, and prayed silently for God to heal him, specifically to clear his nose and take away that horrible cough. Tears pricked at my eyes and then rolled down my cheeks as I prayed. I wasn't sure exactly why I got so emotional, maybe because it was a tender thing to do for my sick little boy. I wanted to speak the words aloud and lay my hand on his head, but I was afraid I'd wake him up.

Later, I repeated my prayer, this time aloud. I had realized that when I had a prayer agenda—specific requests I wanted to bring before God—praying aloud helped tremendously. After all, there's a reason why liturgical prayers have been around for so long. Reciting words aloud to God can help us edit our thoughts and focus better. My head was such a crowded and disorganized place. When I prayed silently, it seemed that my mind would leap off on a tangent before I'd completed even one thought. Perhaps some of this tangentialism was God-led, but I suspected that when my thoughts moved from praise to my grocery list, it was probably more about me than God. Praying aloud helped cut out almost all these extraneous thoughts.

After I asked aloud for God's healing, I decided to add Luther's prayer for good measure. That middle part of the prayer still felt awkward, like I was picking a fight with God, but I couldn't stop thinking about the ending: "Remember, dear heavenly Father, how you have at all times supported and helped your people. I will not stop knocking but will continue crying aloud and pleading to the end of my life. Amen." Luther's words took me back to Matthew 7:7-8: "Ask, and you will receive. Search, and you will find. Knock, and the door will be opened to you. For everyone who asks, receives. Whoever seeks, finds. And to everyone who knocks, the door is opened."

Why couldn't I just ask? Why did I have to overthink everything all the time? Why couldn't I just take it to God and let God decide how to answer or deal with it? All my worries showed was a lack of faith. So I tried to let go of my overthinking and offered two more petitions: for one close friend to get pregnant and for another to find a good mate. I found myself saying "Lord" over and over, in the middle and at the end of every sentence, the kind of repetition that bugs me when I hear myself do it aloud. It's like some sort of evangelical tic. But in that moment it felt right, as a way to focus my thoughts on God.

I continued praying for these three requests, and Ben recovered from his cold. I certainly saw an improvement after I prayed over him at his bedside. That prayer had felt powerful in a way my previous prayers hadn't. I also found out that the friend I had prayed would find a mate went on a date a few days later. But there didn't seem to be any long-term results for him or for my friend hoping to conceive, which I guess wasn't really all that surprising. After all, with both of those requests I had disregarded Foster's advice about starting small.

I had struggled so much with what to ask that I found praying for people without words to be particularly helpful. Instead of asking for something specific, I simply pictured them with God's light and peace shining on them.

Just the act of praying, however, had helped me overcome some of my doubts about the purpose of prayer and some of my worries about praying the wrong thing. Like so many other practices, it was the doing that mattered, not the dithering around about doing it properly. The more I did it, the less I worried about doing it wrong.

I had to stop categorizing my prayer practice as a success or a failure. (And for that matter, I needed to stop applying those labels to myself.) Just because a time of prayer didn't result in a nice neat answer or a deep theological insight didn't mean God wasn't using that time to work in me or do other work I wasn't even aware of. As Evelyn Underhill writes about prayer, "It is quite possible to obtain spiritual nourishment without being consciously aware of it."

Despite my doubts about the why and how of asking, I had never wavered in my conviction that prayer had the power to change *me*, and petitionary prayer was a particularly powerful method. The more seeking and knocking I did, the more naturally it came and the more petitions God seemed to bring to my attention. Petitionary prayer appeared to be not only necessary but healthy for me, since it forced me to focus on other people's needs. In fact, I realized that contemplative prayer, the Examen, and petitionary prayer had all helped me shift my focus from myself to God.

Perhaps more important, these prayers helped me get over my own propensity to worry rather than do.

So many of us spend more time feeling guilty about not praying than we actually spend praying. What if, every time we thought about God or prayer, instead of feeling guilty about not doing it more, we just prayed? What if, instead of worrying about the type of prayer or whether we're doing it right, we just prayed?

Virtually all personal correspondence begins with an apology for not writing sooner. When you receive a letter or an e-mail, do you want to dwell on how long it's been since the person wrote and their reasons for not doing so, or are you just excited to hear from them and to read the letter? Which way do you think God feels when we reach out in prayer, even after a long absence?

The people who are best at prayer almost universally advise us to stop feeling bad about it. Yes, we will forget, but Thomas R. Kelly, in *A Testament of Devotion*, recommends that we just forgive ourselves and move on. Brother Lawrence says that when his attention was drawn away from God, that God simply recalled it not with punishment but with a delightful sensation, and Brother Lawrence was only too happy to comply, remembering how miserable he had felt without God.

When you think of God, pray. Eventually, it becomes a habit.

21

Non-Expert Tips for Practicing Prayer

1. Plan to do it when you're at your best, and if that's at 2 a.m., then you'll probably have a nice uninterrupted prayer time.

2. Start with just a few minutes in God's presence. Really. And if you can do thirty minutes the first time, I don't want to know about it.

3. Try not to judge your results too much. Well, try not to.

4. If you are worried about having the right words to bring a petition before God, just picture God's light and peace shining over that person.

5. If you forget for a day or a week or a month, just forgive yourself and try again. God will still be there.

6. Stop obsessing about it. Just do it. Repeat.

2

FELLOWSHIP: LETTING OTHERS IN

February

Without community our hearts close up and die.
—Jean Vanier

Fellowship seemed like a strange discipline to practice, almost a freebie. After all, was it really necessary to be that intentional about just being with others? I was with other people (okay, Ben) all the time. What I longed for, most of the time, was to be alone.

And there was the rub.

Christianity is meant to be a life lived together, and I was instead becoming more and more well-versed in the art of being alone. For several years now, I'd been working at home, which suited me just fine. Turned out I was a classic introvert, the kind who got worn out being around other people and needed to be alone to recharge.

Yet I'd seen the repercussions of a lack of fellowship. When Ben was born, we'd lived in San Diego only a year and I had very few friends, none of whom had children. The depression I underwent shortly after his birth seemed to have been made darker by this lack of community.

Some of my spiritual desperation also seemed related to my isolation. I was reminded of the truth of German theologian and World War II martyr Dietrich Bonhoeffer's words in *Life Together*:

The Christian needs another Christian who speaks God's Word to him. He needs him again and again when he becomes uncertain and discouraged, for by himself he cannot help himself without belying the truth. He needs his brother man as a bearer and proclaimer of the divine word of salvation. He needs his brother solely because of Jesus Christ. The Christ in his own heart is weaker than the Christ in the word of his brother; his own heart is uncertain, his brother's is sure. And that also clarifies the goal of all Christian community: they meet one another as bringers of the message of salvation.

I wanted to have this kind of community, to have friends who could speak God's word to me, and I to them. To this end, I decided to pursue fellowship on three different levels. First, I would accept any and all invitations to be in fellowship with other mothers. Second, I would engage deliberately in fellowship with my extended family. And third, I would pursue fellowship through the church community we had just joined. After three years of attending several different local churches, Ryan and I had finally joined a church right down the street, and I was excited to become more a part of the life of the church.

Mom Fellowship

A few months after having Ben, I had sought out other moms, if just to preserve a small veneer of sanity by having other people to alternately obsess with and seek reassurance from. I found this fellowship in a local group called Stroller Strides. At Stroller Strides, new moms bonded over the daily celebration of managing to dress both ourselves and our babies and make it out of the house and to a local park. There we jogged up and down the sidewalk and sang to our babies while trying to return our exhausted and unfamiliar bodies back to their pre-pregnancy conditions. The exercise was often secondary to the conversation.

Meeting up with these other moms several mornings a week had formed a lifeline for me, but after a couple of years, almost all of us moved on. Some of us went back to work, others started sending their children to preschool, and others, including me, moved away, in my family's case to a different part of San Diego. One by one, most of these intense friendships faded as suddenly and completely as they had bloomed, and I was back to my fairly solitary existence again.

What with conflicting naptimes, illnesses, and the general inability we all felt to plan ahead more than three minutes, I rarely managed to see even other moms I considered good friends. When we did meet up, kids in tow, we often joked that we started twenty conversations and finished none as we supervised, provided snacks, and broke up spats between our little ones. Plus, now that the early desperation of motherhood had somewhat abated, and I felt reasonably sure that I was not putting Ben in mortal danger on a daily (or even hourly) basis, those mom friendships seemed risky as well as rewarding. Every connection I made was accompanied by all these potential judgments she would make about me (and, let's face it, I would make about her): Were you breastfeeding too long or not long enough? Were you using the right brand of diapers and baby food? Were you too far on the hippie-ish attachment side or the Type-A schedule side of the parenting spectrum? And on and on . . . I found it easier sometimes just not to bother.

But I was determined now to make the effort. My first event was a children's concert at the local library. The place was jam-packed with over-excited kids, strollers, and mommies who, like me, had applied makeup and donned clean shirts for the occasion. Ben and I ended up perched on the edge of a carpet square, smack in the middle of a group of moms who all seemed to know one another. I didn't know a one of them.

Around the corners of the room, however, I could see people I knew slightly. I thought I should probably go say hi to one or the other of them, but then the concert started up, saving me from having to make the effort. Ben seemed as socially paralyzed as I was, sitting like a statue in my lap for several songs, not even wanting to clap. Then all of a sudden he spotted a girl from his preschool class, leaped up, and marched down the rows to sit next to her. They didn't say a word to each other that I saw, but they both seemed happy to be seated together. I, on the other hand, stayed put, not managing to strike up a conversation with anyone new and realizing that I'd allotted only a few minutes to talk with some of the moms I did know after the concert before I had to run home to meet the babysitter. Fellowship for two-year-olds seemed to be significantly less complex than fellowship for their tightly wound, over-scheduled, and stressed-out moms.

The very next day, I was supposed to meet a new acquaintance from church for lunch, but I was getting over a cold, so I canceled. By lunchtime I felt much better and started second-guessing my decision. It was clear that when in doubt, my first instinct was to cancel, and I couldn't deny that I'd felt relieved about not having to go. It seemed like so much work to get there and try to wrangle Ben while engaging in a thoughtful conversation. Much easier to just stay home with him where he could run around and be loud.

It was one of the strangest ways motherhood was isolating. Ben was in so many ways a wonderful companion. I never anticipated how fulfilling everyday kinds of interactions like talking to him in the grocery store or going on a walk together would be. In a way, I hadn't realized how much I missed having someone to talk to until I had someone to interact with constantly.

Yet, at the same time, his constant presence prevented me from connecting in a deep way with other adults. So although I was rarely alone, I still felt lonely much of the time.

And as I continued praying the Examen, I kept seeing the truth of Bonhoeffer's words about Christ in other people. I realized that although I regularly felt I saw Christ in Ben or Ryan or sometimes in nature, I also frequently saw Christ in other people I encountered—from preschool, from church, or just from the grocery store. Not to put too fine a point on it, but it seemed clear that if I didn't create or at least respond to opportunities to spend time with other people, I would be missing out on a lot of Christ.

Letting Others In

So I persisted with the next item on my mom fellowship offensive: attending the first meeting of a book club that was part of the MOPS (Mothers of Preschoolers) group at our new church. I booked Ryan well in advance, and to our equal relief, he wasn't delayed at the office, so I was not only on time for once (timeliness is not one of my great virtues), I was the first one there. I had a great time chatting with the host before the others arrived. The experience reminded me of how I'd brought Ben early to his children's dance class so he could get used to being in the space by himself and not cling to me so much when all the other kids arrived. Apparently, the early arrival technique was equally effective for me. It was slightly humiliating to think that I needed the same social strategies as an eighteen-month-old, but hey, any port in a storm.

Ladies trickled in, most with stories about the disasters that had delayed their arrival. These stories were ubiquitous to any gathering of mothers; inevitably many involved poop. After sharing anecdotes, we actually started talking about the book, William Young's *The Shack*, which only a few of us had managed to read. I had finished the book and was pretty excited to share some of my thoughts. After all, books! Writing! God! These were my areas! But right away one woman started to rub me the wrong way. She knew *all about* the book; she kept interrupting others to lecture about her own ideas. In the interest of my fellowship practice, I tried to step back and figure out why she bugged me so much, and the answer was depressing. *I* wanted to be the one who knew all about the book. *I* wanted to be the one who knew the most about theology and was the authority when others had questions. In other words, I wasn't much interested in listening; I wanted to talk. I'd been thinking of fellowship as finding some people to talk to, and in doing so, had left out the key part of the equation.

Most of us are better talkers than listeners. Sometimes I wonder who we're all talking to, since when silent so many of us seem to be just waiting for our turn to talk. Good listening requires not just silence and attention but also interest and even a little bit of humility, a respect for the person who is talking and a recognition that he or she has knowledge and experience that you do not. That part can be difficult. There is such a thing as good talking, too, or at least talking that leads to fellowship. It is characterized by vulnerability, the willingness to reveal yourself as you really are. You can lecture all you want and not reveal a single truth about yourself, but good talking requires honesty. It tends to be rooted in personal experience. A back-and-forth of listening and talking, marked by a mutual vulnerability and openness, is at the heart of not only good conversation but also good fellowship. After all, how can someone else speak Christ's words to you if you don't let them in? Or even let them speak?

That night, I tried to think more about listening than sharing my own insights and ended up feeling that I'd learned quite a bit. Hearing some of the other women's reactions to the book and how it reminded them of traumatic experiences in their own lives, I could also see the truth of something Dallas Willard writes about: that God can be more present, and present in a more concentrated way, among a group. By myself, I could have thought about that book all day and felt very satisfied with my little insights, but in the group, I received a much fuller picture and one that resulted less in a feeling of satisfaction with myself than in a sense of awe of all that God is and can do.

What Works for Me

Krystee, Navy wife, writer, and mom of two

My husband just received orders to Singapore, and what's made me able to live here is the group of spouses. We got here and no one had their own lives anymore. Through going out together once a month and then getting together individually, we've found a way to talk through some of the things that are hard about living in a foreign country. If one of the women goes into labor early, we're going to take care of her son. Every time we get together at least someone says what a blessing our group is. I've never experienced fellowship like I do right here.

Family Fellowship

A few days later, my parents and mother- and father-in-law arrived in town for Ben's baptism at our new church. I loved their visits but also always found myself exhausted by the pre-visit cleaning and preparation. In the case of my parents in particular, I sometimes wondered why I felt such a need to present them with an immaculate home. They'd lived with me for years; they surely knew that it didn't look that way the rest of the time. Was it just hospitality, as I told myself, or was it more of my trying to present to the world a perfect but false image?

The morning of the baptism we walked the few blocks to church en masse, Ryan and me, Ryan's parents, our friend Jeff, and of course, Ben, the guest of honor. Ben danced all the way there, he was so excited to be surrounded by all of his favorite people and to be the center of attention. When we got close to the church, we saw my parents, who had come straight to the church from their hotel, standing on the steps looking for us, and Ben ran up and launched himself at them, as little boys are wont to do. It was one of those moments where the happiness just smacks you in the face and you feel a little dizzy with the force of it all.

When we gathered at the front of the church for the ceremony, Ben pointed excitedly to the water font and then to his head, to the delight of the audience. Ryan and I might have described the baptism ritual to him one too many times. We grinned like fools and, at least in my case, blinked tears away as our families and the members of the congregation promised to help raise him in the Church. Ben was getting his molars in so throughout the ceremony he chewed on his sleeve, peering out from behind it with a meditative little crease on his brow. I'd thought of the baptism as dedicating Ben to God and as our promise to take good care of this child God had entrusted us with, but the ceremony itself felt so much more communal than I had anticipated. I looked around at all the smiling faces in the pews, many of which I recognized but many more which I did not, and thought about how this was our village, the village that would raise our child. I hoped we had chosen wisely.

Before my in-laws left, my father-in-law taught me to prune my roses. He's a teacher by trade, but I am not always the greatest student, probably because I hate to admit ignorance. This time, however, perhaps because pruning roses was altogether foreign to me and I had no pride whatsoever in my own ability to accomplish this task, I was able to be a better and more open student. I learned a lot from him, our rose branches ended up in beautiful cup shapes, and miracle of miracles, I think we both enjoyed the time very much. Then all the grandparents headed home, except my mom, who stayed on for a few extra days. She's the one I am closest to, the one I talk to the most, and yet in many ways she is the one I have the hardest time getting along with. I am sharp with her like I am with nobody else. She once asked me in a quiet voice why I was so patient with everyone but her. It was an excellent question. I wish I knew the answer.

All I could think was that I'd seen the same pattern with the way Ben sometimes saved his anger, both emotional and physical, for me. It's the moms, the safe ones in our lives, who sometimes bear the brunt of our frustrations. Maybe it's only with those we feel most safe that we can reveal our true selves, even the sides of our selves that aren't so pretty.

Church Fellowship

The beauty of the baptism ceremony had made me more eager to pursue fellowship with our new church community, yet I still found myself ready to cancel these commitments for the slightest reason. When Ben got sick the day we were to volunteer with the fifth- and sixth-grade ministry, I would have stayed home with him if Ryan hadn't practically kicked me out the door. Of course I had a great time. Don't tell Ryan, but he is almost always right about that stuff.

The next week was Holy Week, and just a few minutes before we were going to leave for the Ash Wednesday dinner and service, Ryan called to say that he had to work late and couldn't make it. The idea of going to a church dinner with my two-year-old and sitting with a table of people I probably didn't know without my socially extroverted husband to carry the conversation and help with Ben was daunting. But I had already told Ben all about it, and he was excited so we packed up (like any newish mother, I always traveled Sherpa-like with a fully loaded diaper bag, even on the briefest of errands) and headed out the door.

At the entrance to the Family Life Center, we peeked in and saw beautifully set tables with white tablecloths and a candlelit Communion table in the center. I had expected a casual buffet, with casseroles and paper plates, like a Sunday morning pancake breakfast, so the fancy setup made me hesitate at the door. But our pastor spotted us and quickly ushered us to a table with a retired couple and their two adult daughters. As I sat down, he introduced me by saying that I'd written the book the church home groups were all studying for Lent. They wanted to hear all about that and ended up buying two of the copies that were for sale at a side table and asking me to sign them. I was flattered and embarrassed at the same time. Then this lovely family served us bread and soup and salad and made a fuss over Ben and before I knew it, it was time for the kids to head to the children's program. As I walked him to the nursery, a friend from MOPS reached out to hug us and so did the fifth- and sixth-grade ministry leader, making me feel like a real member of the community, a sense that was reinforced by the way the girls working in the nursery squealed as soon as they saw Ben. He couldn't have been more happy. And I wandered back to the hall and had a pretty good time myself, enjoying an adult conversation about writing and faith.

As I listened to the Lenten message, basking in the candlelight and the feeling of being pleasantly full, stomach and heart, I looked around the table and realized I truly felt I belonged.

I couldn't help but remember that, without the urging of my husband and then my pastor, I would have missed it. A large part of fellowship was fighting my default response of no and just saying yes.

Fellowship, Not Competition

The last day of February, a Saturday, I was looking forward to two fellowship opportunities—a MOPS craft day where I could get some extra writing time in while other moms worked on projects of their own, and a baby shower for one of my friends from Stroller Strides. But on the way to church for the MOPS session, I spilled tea all over the inside of my diaper bag and Ben was in one of those two-year-old moods. He didn't want to walk; he didn't want to be carried; he didn't want to do anything at all. So by the time we walked in the door of the nursery, I was in tears, worrying about my deadline and stewing over how unfair it felt that I had to go to such lengths to get any work done when all Ryan had to do was head to his office. Finally, I got Ben settled and got out my computer, looking forward to getting some work done.

Then one of the other moms asked me if I had Ben enrolled in the church preschool. When I told her yes, she started telling me and the rest of the group about the pros and cons of co-op, Montessori,

Waldorf, and German immersion. I hadn't even considered any of these schools. We'd heard that the preschool at our church was really good, and since it was also within walking distance it had seemed like the obvious choice, but as she talked on and on, I started to panic. Maybe it wasn't good enough. Didn't I want the best for my child? Why hadn't I done more research? What was wrong with me?

I could see the worry lines appearing between the eyes of the others moms in the room, too, as she wound us all up like spools of thread. Needless to say, I didn't manage to get much work done.

As soon as the session ended, I grabbed Ben and speed-walked home to e-mail my mom for the address of a relative who'd been an elementary school librarian, so I could ask her if I should pursue Montessori or Waldorf. I stared at the screen, my stomach churning, wondering if it was too late to even apply. I felt like I'd been injected with some kind of preschool poison that activated all my competitive-mom genes. And now I was running late for my friend's shower, and I still had to pick up a gift for her.

I ended up stopping at Starbucks and buying her a gift card. When I half-jogged into the restaurant, I was thrilled to see two of my other close friends from Stroller Strides. I dived into a seat next to them and whispered that I only had time to grab a Starbucks card for a gift and I hoped it was okay. They both loudly assured me that it was perfect. One told me she hadn't even had time to get a card; she'd just wrapped up a big pack of diapers and wrote our friend's name on it with a Sharpie. I felt myself relax by degrees every minute that I sat there. It was my own fault, I realized. I didn't have to get all wound up over preschools when I'd made a perfectly good decision on my own. I didn't have to be so sure I knew everything that I freaked out when somebody else wanted to share or just disagreed with me.

I realized that my efforts at fellowship were consistently sabo-taged by my own sense of competitiveness and its companion, my rush to judge others. I was so concerned about being perceived as a good mom—or even a perfect mom—that I was reluctant to take any steps toward fellowship that might dispel that perception.

Dutch priest Henri Nouwen believed our increasing prosperity has led to our increasing isolation, the "bowling alone" phenomenon, if you will. He writes:

Success has isolated a lot of people and made them lonely. It seems sometimes as though meetings between people generally happen on the way to something or someone else. There's always some-thing else more important, more pressing, of more consequence. The ordinary, simple, little, homely things have to make way for something you really ought to be doing: that film you really should see, the country you simply must visit, and this or that events which you've got to attend. And the higher up you get on the ladder of prosperity, the harder it becomes to be together, to sing together, and to celebrate life together in a spirit of thanksgiving.

My own ideas about prosperity and success had led to this very mind-set he described. I was so worried about what people thought about me or about Ben and how I was parenting him that I was unable to enjoy those ordinary, simple gifts of fellowship. I could be free of that only with people who already knew me, with whom I didn't have to pretend that I wasn't a flawed mess—my extended family, Ryan, those mom friends who'd seen me at my early morning and anxious worst. It was difficult to form a relationship like this in a group set-ting, which is probably why I'd discovered that one-on-one interac-tions seemed to produce a lot more meaningful sense of fellowship for me. It would take continuing effort on my part to create more relationships like that.

But in the meantime, I had the freedom to take a look at the impossible image I wanted to project of myself and try to let it go. After all, no one could compete with me unless I let them. It took fellowship, over something as trivial as a Starbucks card and a pack of diapers, to show me that. Just as Bonhoeffer pointed out, true friends can speak God's word to us like that, much more effectively than we can tell ourselves.

Non-Expert Tips for Practicing Fellowship

1. If you tend toward introversion, work on saying yes, even when you don't think you want to. Remind yourself that just about every time you force your reluctant self out of the house, you enjoy yourself.

2. Seek out the ways in which you connect best with others, whether that is one-on-one, in small groups, or in larger groups.

3. Remember to listen.

4. Show your true self, not yourself as you want to be. You cannot have real fellowship with anyone unless you let your guard down.

3

SUBMISSION:
RELAXING INTO GOD'S WILL

March

When we think we can do it all ourselves—fix, save, buy, or date a nice
solution—it's hopeless. We're going to screw things up. We're going to
get our tentacles wrapped around things and squirt our squiddy ink all
over, so that there is even less visibility, and then we're going to squeeze
the very life out of everything.

—Anne Lamott, *Help, Thanks, Wow*

Jesus told his followers to deny themselves, take up their crosses, and follow him. In spiritual formation language, this self-denial is known as *submission*. Submission to God's will, to the Bible, to those around us. This sounds good when I read it—yes, of course I want to do God's will, but when I think about actually trying to put it into practice . . . yuck. Who wants *not* to be in charge of anything? I don't think there has ever been a discipline I dreaded practicing more than submission. Prayer—yes! Fellowship—okay! But as the calendar turned to March, I felt myself fighting my own plan to practice submission. I told myself it was too hard; that I should do other, easier disciplines first; that I submitted too much already in my daily life of being a mom and wife, even in my job.

It didn't help that submission is such a loaded term. If you're submissive, then someone else is dominating you, and why would you want that? Yet it's more complicated than that. Here is the definition of *submission* from *The Life with God Bible* (a study Bible with an emphasis on the spiritual disciplines), and it is a doozy:

> Subordination to the guidance of God; within the Christian fellowship, a constant mutual subordination out of reverence for Christ, which opens the way for particular subordination to those who are qualified to direct our efforts toward Christlikeness and who then add the weight of their wise authority on the side of our willing spirit to help us do the things we would like to do and refrain from doing the things we don't want to do.

The reason this definition is so long and unwieldy is that Foster and the other editors of *The Life with God Bible* are anxious that submission not be abused or misunderstood, that no one be taken advantage of. In no other discipline is there so much chance for abuse and potential damage.

These were serious concerns, but I had to admit that they didn't have much to do with my real problem with submission. I wasn't stuck in an unhealthy relationship—far from it—my husband's motto is "Happy wife, happy life." No, the problem for me was my old friend, the will. My will, my self-interest, the part of me that wanted to get my own way all the time, had been seriously thwarted by motherhood, and it wasn't very happy about it. Simply put, I felt like I was submitting too much already. Not in an unhealthy way, just that I was already sick of submitting to everyone else's priorities and schedules and preferences, and I wasn't even *trying* to practice submission.

All this reluctance couldn't, however, obscure the fact that all along I knew that submission was the discipline I was being called to practice this month. Finally, I reread the chapter on submission in

Celebration of Discipline. I had forgotten how appealing Foster made submission sound, describing it as the "freedom" of letting go of our own wants and needs. But in the end I was convinced by the idea that the point of submission is to teach us that following one's own will is *not* the path to happiness.

The goal I set for myself was to practice submission in my interpersonal relationships and interactions, and also in my relationship with God, to try not to resist what I heard as God's will for me. Yes, I could understand that God's will for me was superior to my own—at least in theory; it was the first part I most wanted to resist. Sometimes I felt as though, as a mom especially, but also as a wife, all I did was put my own needs aside for Ben and Ryan. I didn't get to do what I wanted, eat what I wanted, go where I wanted, even use the bathroom without an audience, because I was trying to do what they wanted, to give them what they needed. Until I started reflecting on the practice of submission, I hadn't realized how deeply ingrained in me this idea was. I was operating on a sense of "Mom as martyr," who let everyone else have his or her way. Poor Mom.

But the truth was that my perspective was a little skewed. Most of the time I made Ben bow to my agenda, as was appropriate because if he were in charge, he might do nothing but eat chocolate and watch *Thomas & Friends* all day. I am not blind to the parallel here in my relationship with God. Of course God knows better than I do what is truly good for me and what will truly make me happy, and as much as I might think it is reading novels on the beach all day, he knows and even I know, deep down, that is not the path to happiness and contentment. I appreciate that God keeps pointing out this truth to me, mostly gently.

Case in point. One morning, Ben woke up cranky and acting tired. Since he had been sick so often these last few months, my first thought was that he was getting sick again. I asked him if he wanted to go to school, and he yelled, "No!" I was a bit taken aback by his emphatic response. Since he didn't have a fever or any other worrying symptoms, I suggested to him that instead of preschool I'd just take him to Stroller Strides class and he could rest or sleep in the stroller while I kept an eye on him. He thought that sounded like a great idea, so I changed into my workout clothes. A few minutes later, he came into the bathroom where I was getting ready and announced that he didn't want to go to Stroller Strides. He wanted to go to school, and he emphasized his preference by pitching a little fit, complete with the Weeping of Crocodile Tears and the Throwing of Board Books. Clearly, he was feeling better. I said, "OK, we can go to school then," and started to change back into my jeans. He started to cry again, and announced he didn't want to go to school after all. So I put my workout clothes back on and said, "Let's go to Stroller Strides!" His response? Yes, you guessed it. Another fit. "*I want to go to school! I want to see my friends!*"

By this point it was almost 9:30, half an hour past the start of school and almost too late to make it to the 9:30 Stroller Strides class. What was going on with him? Was he really sick? Was he just too tired? Finally, it dawned on me that it was ridiculous and probably unfair to be laying this decision at his feet. He needed me to decide whether he was going to school or to Stroller Strides and then to just tell him. So I put my jeans back on—by now I felt like we were shooting a dressing room scene in a movie—and took him to school.

By the time we got there, it was almost an hour into the preschool morning. As we entered the courtyard, he broke into a trot and made a beeline for his classroom door. His classmates were seated around the table for snack, and he jumped right in and claimed a seat. A short time later, when I picked him up, one of his teachers told me that he had chattered happily all morning about how glad he was to be at school. I felt like an idiot. Why hadn't I just brought him in the first place? I felt God's whisper in my mind: *Yes, Julia, it's appropriate for him to be submissive because that's what's best for him most of the time. He simply doesn't have all the information he needs to make most decisions on his own.* Hmmmm. That sounded familiar.

What Do *You* Want to Do?

My first attempts at actually practicing submission came when my sister, brother-in-law, and their two daughters came to visit. Submission within family relationships is an interesting part of this whole process. In my family we can all sit around being nice for a while and saying, "I don't care. Let's do what you want to do," and then the one who usually decides is my mom, who on the surface of things is the most submissive of us all. She tends to be the most "I don't care," at least until we come to a decision that she is not crazy about, and then it turns out she might care just the slightest little bit. As Foster points out, sometimes when we say we don't care, what we are actually saying is that we do care very much.

So in their visit, I tried to be submissive to their will. This mainly took the form of presenting options I thought they would enjoy for outings or dinner or whatever, and then just sitting back and letting them decide rather than force-marching everyone around town according to my personal San Diego itinerary. I found submission in this context not to be about never leading or making a decision. After all, this was my home turf, so a certain amount of that was required. Instead, I found myself needing to let go of having to be the expert, of having to be right about everything. In other words, I tried not to hold the responsibility for everyone's potential happiness so tightly in my grip. Turns out that is very freeing. If you assign yourself as head decision-maker and things don't go well, you take it so personally, and if things do go well, you take it personally in an equally unpleasant way, giving yourself much more credit than is due. (At least *I* do that.) So trying to just facilitate a nice visit for my family without forcing my own will or opinions on them too much was surprisingly fun and rewarding. Just letting go a little bit of having to have my own way helped me enjoy everything so much more.

The day they left, however, I found myself eagerly anticipating doing something I really wanted to do. Just me, nobody else. The minute Ben went down for his nap, I started to play a movie on my laptop, a documentary called *My Child Could Paint That!* even though I was usually extremely strict with myself about using his naptime for work. After just a short time of consciously practicing submission, it felt so decadent to do whatever I wanted. The will is strong. It reasserts itself very, very fast.

Getting Out of God's Way

One area in which I consistently struggle with submitting is my work. I fret about meeting my deadlines, and as much as I try to plan, I always seem to be behind. I had set a goal for myself of finishing three *A Year with God* sections per week for the month, and at the end of the very first week I had three started but none completed.

Enter the worry and second-guessing. My inability to meet my own writing goals is likely related to my less-than-organized writing style. I throw a lot of time at whatever I am doing, and then just when I start to despair, suddenly I am done. Don't ask me how I know when I'm done. I just do. As William Shawn, legendary editor of the *New Yorker*, used to say, "It takes as long as it takes." You'd think after writing and editing for so many years I'd be better at predicting how long each job takes me, but I don't seem to be. Even though I know I work a lot more quickly at the end of projects as I get into a groove, this pattern of always feeling behind creates a lot of stress in my life as I become more and more convinced I'll never meet my deadline and then somehow I usually do. Sometimes I wish my subconscious would let the rest of me in on the secret.

God was certainly aware of how much work I had. As long as I didn't take on any extra stuff, I felt that submission in this part of my life meant asking God for help and then refusing to lose my mind over it. Yet as sensible and appealing as that sounded, in practice it proved difficult. I knew that this mind-set was less about handing over control than just acknowledging that God already had control, but it still felt scary to admit to not being in charge. And I struggled with the details. After all, I obviously had a lot of say here in how late I stayed up and just how much of the housework I ignored to grab extra work time. To put it baldly, where did I draw the line between trusting God and forcing myself to keep staying up all night? It was unclear.

I realized one concrete way I could demonstrate submission in this area was to try to spend time with Ben without thinking about my writing. When I got behind in work, I tended to think about little else, even during non-work time. Not only was that unfair to Ben, it didn't get the book written any faster. I wondered if I really could forget about work during playtime, but to my surprise just giving myself permission to do it seemed to be enough. Despite my failure to complete my first three sections that first week, I was able to put that aside and just play yard baseball with Ben.

This focus on play was as good for me as it was for him because the truth was that I was tired of working on this project for so long. As an unexpected bonus, taking a break seemed to help me focus better when I did work.

Submitting Through Silence

While I was trying to put into practice the idea of submission in my work, another area where submission seemed to be called for was in the every-other-week Young Marrieds group we'd just started attending at church. This season, the group happened to be discussing the Bible study I had co-written, and I dreaded the thought of hearing people critique my ideas and my theology. I realized that I was spending an inordinate amount of time anticipating things people *might* say and getting annoyed by those imaginary comments and even thinking up defenses for them. Such a practice, when examined, seemed just shy of, well, insane.

Even if some of the people in my group did have a problem with some of the things I'd written, I decided to do my best to listen and not try to defend myself or the material. Building on my fellowship experiences, I wanted to open myself up to learning from others, and that was hard to do when I was arguing with them in my head or planning a clever comment. It was clear to me what submission meant in this context—shutting up. And its corollary, trying to humbly learn from the others in the group.

I found that, in working to set aside my defensiveness, I paid much closer attention to what everyone said. In thinking less about what I planned to say, I was free to listen to and learn from everyone else. Several times responses bubbled up in me, but I decided there on the spot that I could contribute only three times, so I concluded that most of those thoughts really weren't worth sharing—for instance, I wanted to make a comment about Ramadan when one woman spoke about her fasting practice, but what I wanted to say wasn't based on my own experiences, just something I'd observed in others, and I thought my goal for sharing it might have been showing off. Plus, I didn't really see how it could help anyone else in the room. So I kept my mouth shut. And I learned something from everyone there that night.

The study group represented a kind of high-water mark of my submission practice that month. Soon after, I caught yet another cold and could no longer manage to give God my worries over my monthly deadline. Of the final nine sections I had to do that month, it had taken me more than a week to get through just the first one, which was on guidance. I kept veering from panic and fatigue to a terrible sense of foreboding that I would have to tell my editor I had not met my deadline.

What Works for Me

Tanya, pharmacist and mother of three

It's an intense season of life, having three small children, and at times I wish I had more time to take care of all my needs and wants. But submitting to the season I'm in means embracing the tasks joyfully and gratefully rather than begrudgingly. This season won't last forever and when it's gone, I'm pretty sure I'll miss it. So I try to inhabit the present, savoring the special moments, and the challenges, and deliberately submitting to this privilege God has given me to be a mother.

In keeping with my efforts to practice submission, however, I kept telling myself that I had to give up control of the project. I had to submit to God—trusting that either God would help me get it done or I just wouldn't get it done. I had struggled with the balance between where I needed to trust God to work with the time I gave to the project and where I just needed to buckle down and carve out more time, but I'd now come to the point where I simply didn't have any extra hours to spare. All I could do was work as hard as I could within the allotted time I had. Where I had to trust, where I had to place myself in God's hands, was in what I accomplished when I sat down to work. Sounds simple, but this idea was a novel approach for me, and one I found strangely freeing and calming. There was no way I could work while I was grocery shopping with Ben or cleaning the house or walking the dog, so what was the point of worrying about work while I did those things?

The worst thing that could happen would be that I would have to admit to my editors that I couldn't do it. This was a tremendous fear of mine, yet that month I thought about having to do that so many times it finally seemed less scary.

Facing up to the worst-case scenario robs it of some of its power. And helps you realize how much time you waste worrying about it. Worrying about meeting a deadline has never yet helped me meet one. On the contrary, worrying is extremely time-consuming.

But then just when I started to feel a little smug about my new feeling of acceptance, panic set in again. I had planned to do a lot of work over the weekend, and when the Sunday night dust settled, I hadn't finished even half of what I'd planned. I felt like I was back at square one again with submission, panicky and exhausted. Life continued to get in the way of my work. My cold was getting worse and our busy weekend—guests for dinner Saturday, other guests for lunch Sunday, and yet more guests for dinner Sunday—hadn't helped. Monday afternoon Ben's teacher called me after class to report that he had a runny nose and seemed "out of sorts" all morning. Sick *again*. I couldn't believe it.

All of a sudden it seemed health was our family's central preoccupation.

Submitting to the Frailty of the Body

Another topic I'd been studiously avoiding thinking about was Ryan's upcoming surgery. It was a planned procedure to alleviate, hopefully permanently, a condition called *achalasia* in which the esophagus doesn't close properly, resulting in reflux and discomfort. The surgery would take several hours and then he would need to remain in the hospital for at least a couple of nights. Ryan's parents had come down to stay with Ben so I could be at the hospital with Ryan as much as possible.

The morning of the surgery, Ryan and I had planned to go to breakfast together. He wouldn't be able to eat, but he wanted us to have a few minutes to talk. But then some last-minute work came up and by the time he was ready to go, it was late enough that we had to go straight to the hospital for check-in. As nurses came and examined Ryan, gave him a gown to change into, and asked him the usual questions about his medications and when he had last eaten, I started to feel overheated and light-headed.

I knew what that feeling meant.

Ever since high school, I've been a fainter. Every once in a while, in times of stress or extreme fatigue, I just wilt like the Southern belle I otherwise am not. Not eating or drinking was a trigger. So was anxiety, like the sort I was feeling over Ryan's procedure. It was ridiculous. Here was Ryan, preparing for surgery and restricted from eating since the previous night, and I'm the one ready to pass out on the floor.

Feeling increasingly hot and dizzy, I rifled through my bag for something to eat and came up with nothing. Honestly, the *one* time I wasn't hauling my snack-filled diaper bag. . . . Then I felt the black curtain start to fall across my vision, a sure sign I was about to drop. I did the only thing I could. I quickly lowered myself to the floor and stretched out flat, resting my cheek on the cold tile. I hadn't yet mentioned to Ryan how I was feeling, so my new posture required some explaining.

To his immense credit, he refrained from rolling his eyes and was instead just concerned about getting me something to eat, but I wouldn't let him tell anyone what had happened. Yes, it was unbelievably embarrassing, but mostly I was terrified a nurse would take one look at me and I'd end up on a gurney with an IV in my arm.

So I tried to make myself very small there on the floor, peering under the curtains for approaching feet and trying not to think about what might have been on that tile where I was resting my cheek. Ryan peeked out and asked about vending machines and we found out the closest food was a few floors down. For the moment anyway, I wasn't going anywhere. And neither was Ryan, already suited up in his hospital gown. We didn't quite know what to do. It was funny and sad and humiliating.

I had no choice but to submit, this time to the embarrassing frailty of my body. I hated the thought of taking medical attention away from Ryan, but it didn't seem like there was any other option.

Just then, completely out of the blue, our friend Jeff texted me and said he was there at the hospital. Completely unbeknownst to us, he had remembered it was Ryan's surgery day and decided to drop in and see him beforehand. What an unbelievable blessing. I explained to him that I needed something to eat, and he was able to put his hands on a muffin before joining us in the room. I have never been so glad to see a cellophane-wrapped pastry in my life. Not to mention Jeff.

A few bites of the food revived me enough to get me off the floor, luckily before the doctor came in to talk to us about the procedure, and then it was time for me to leave Ryan. Jeff headed to work, and I set up my laptop at a table in the waiting area. The surgery was scheduled to take several hours, so I worked away. The section I was working on that day was about chastity. It seemed slightly ironic to be writing about that when my husband was undergoing surgery, and I had to face the chance that something could go wrong and I might lose him. How could I submit to something like that?

The surgery went perfectly, to my great relief, and by the time Ryan was in recovery, I had written an entire section, placing me, believe it or not, on target for my deadline. I was just happy to sit in the room with him as he dozed in anesthetized sleep. One day I would have to submit to losing him, or to leaving him behind, but not today.

Life requires an awful lot of submission from all of us. Our bodies get sick, at some point for many of us our minds fail, and eventually we all die. We don't get any choice in these matters.

It seems to me that it's these big areas where we have to submit that lead us to cling so tightly to the small things we can control. It's one of the hardest things about being a child, the feeling that you don't get to control much of anything. When adults see Ben riding in his stroller, they often comment how much they'd love if someone would push them around that way. For kids, of course, being trapped in the stroller is often the last thing they want.

And yet perhaps we should tell ourselves, as I'm always telling my son, "Relax!" I want him to trust me, to trust that I know where we're going and that I'm watching over him on the journey.

Plus, the ride is so much more enjoyable if you stop struggling against the straps. Instead of working within God's perfect will, within the small areas we do get to control, we bring so much additional anxiety upon ourselves by trying desperately to control the rest of it. When I can do it, when I can relax into God's will, everything works so much better.

During those (frequent) times when my life seems out of control, and I want to exert some control over it, I often remind myself of what a wise woman from my MOPS group once told me—that it's all or nothing with motherhood. If you want the children, you also get the moments where you're peeing with an audience or your beloved son is pelting you with cereal from the backseat or dinner is frozen chicken nuggets because naptime prevented you from getting to the grocery store or your child is really, truly sick and you're so scared you can't stop shaking. Do you want it all or do you want none of it?

I want the all, of course. I'm strapped in, and I'm doing my best to submit, trust God, and enjoy the ride.

Non-Expert Tips for Practicing Submission

1. Don't be so afraid of letting someone else, namely God, be in charge. After all, are you doing that great of a job at it?

2. View mutual submission to those around you, in the sense of respecting and bowing to their opinions and preferences, as an act of love.

3. In recognition of the time- and soul-sucking qualities of worry, try to trust God instead. Keep trying.

4. Relax and enjoy this season of life. Ask anyone whose kids are grown—when it's gone, you're going to miss it.

4

STUDY: BUILDING A FIRM FOUNDATION

April

Reading, studying, memorizing, and meditating upon Scripture has always been the foundation of the Christian disciplines.
—*The Life with God Bible*

One of my favorite things about my work is that it gives me lots of opportunities to read the Bible. Of course there is a difference between reading passages for work (as devotional and educational as that can be) and reading passages for your own private study time with God. I had actually planned to try meditation (or meditative reading) in April—reading brief Bible passages very slowly and with plenty of time for reflection. But then I went to hear Lee Strobel, journalist and author of *The Case for Christ* (among many other books), speak about the evidence within the biblical record for Jesus' resurrection, and I changed my mind. It was not meditation over Scripture that I needed; it was study—the more analytical process of reading, inhabiting, and seeking to interpret Scripture rather than immediately apply it to our own lives. Plus, I'd always remembered Richard Foster's words that what Christians today most needed was the study of long passages of Scripture.

I couldn't argue with that.

With the possible exception of prayer, Bible study (or the lack thereof) is the discipline Christians feel most guilty about. And despite the time I spent in my Bible for work, I was no exception. Not surprisingly, the Bible tells us that we should spend a lot of time reading and thinking about the Bible. The kings of Israel were explicitly directed to always have a copy of the law nearby and to read it daily. The Psalms get a lot more inspirational about it: "Great are the works of the LORD, / studied by all who delight in them," wrote the psalmist (111:2 NRSV).

That focus on study, and also the delight, used to come more effortlessly to me. One of the reasons I chose the life path I did was that I wanted to fit Bible study somehow into my career. I was a religion major as an undergraduate and then decided to pursue a masters in theological studies. I remember walking home after class my first semester in seminary, all these little thoughts about God and the world bursting pleasurably like champagne bubbles in my brain and thinking, *How amazing is it that* my job *right now is to study this stuff?*

When I was studying the Bible for my undergrad and graduate classes, I felt that every detail and discovery was interesting not only from a tetchy little academic point of view but also in terms of a life application point of view. Even when I studied or learned things that challenged my faith as I had previously understood it (and this happens to every student of theology), I was still engaged and fascinated by the process. Most of all, I was convinced of the essentialness of the endeavor.

I wanted to get back to that place. Trouble was, it was harder when I wasn't outwardly motivated by school or work or even a church-led Bible study. Oh, it wasn't that I didn't read. One of the most dire warnings I'd ever received about life after baby was that I'd never be able to read again. That hit me harder than all the stuff about lack of sleep and permanent baby weight. I could not imagine my life without reading.

And it turned out that I was able to work it in just fine. I managed to prop a book under the nursing pillow when Ben was a baby. I read while I was cooking and brushing my teeth (I apologize to the public library for this). Bottom line: you fit in what you most want to fit in. My house was a mess, but I kept up with my reading.

And yet it wasn't my Bible I was carting around the kitchen. It was usually a novel or a magazine. Why didn't I gravitate more to the Bible? For one thing, novels offered a bit of escapism. I liked reading novels that were similar to my experience—mommy-lit-type stuff where I could relate to the characters but at the same time enjoy their extreme high jinks without having to suffer the consequences, and novels about lives that couldn't be further from my own—thrillers, police procedurals, mysteries. Both offered a bit of enjoyment and relief. Magazines I read for parenting and home advice and news. The Bible didn't feel so escapist or, despite my faith, so directly helpful.

Theologian Daniel Hames lists three reasons why Christians don't read their Bibles. First, we *say* we don't have enough time. Second, we expect the Bible to give us tips for life, like a parenting magazine, and fail to appreciate that it is really not about us but about our life with God. Hames's third reason why we don't read our Bibles is that we mistakenly believe that Bible reading is for God's sake, not our own— that God wants us to do it, and so we should. For God.

Hames suggests we should instead think of not reading the Bible as simply missing an opportunity to take advantage of God's good gift, rather than feeling guilty about displeasing God. That rang true. I realized that I spent a lot of time thinking about whether I was disappointing God by not practicing more disciplines, especially Bible reading.

So I decided to embark on celebrating more of God's good gift of the Bible by reading through all four of the Gospels and Romans.

(I had just co-authored a study guide on Acts, so I felt pretty well-versed in that one at the moment.) My idea, inspired by Foster's comment about Christians needing to read long passages, was to get through great swaths of my Bible that month. Wasn't that just typical of me? Why read just one Gospel when I could gallop through all four and a bonus book besides? I didn't worry too much about the how of my plan. I just planned to grab the Bible that was always at my desk and read through it when I was taking a break from work. (Looking back at my track record, I probably should have known better.)

I'd like to report that I read through all five books, but I'll just tell you now before you think this chapter is going to last for ten years: I didn't even finish Matthew.

Genealogies and Baptisms

The first day, I enthusiastically began with Matthew's genealogy of Jesus' ancestry, that list of who begat whom from Abraham all the way to Joseph. I usually viewed lineages as something to skim, but this time I found myself fascinated by the few women's names and the less-than-lovely biblical history they demonstrated. Rahab, the prostitute who saved Joshua's men from death in Jericho (see Judges 2–6), is listed here as the mother of Boaz, who married Ruth, another famous biblical woman (although a less obviously sinful one). Jesus is listed as being descended from David through Solomon, whose mother was "the wife of Uriah"—Bathsheba, although she is not named. How incredible that the genealogical line resulting from David's greatest fall from grace (committing adultery with Bathsheba and having her husband, Uriah, killed in battle) was the one from which God chose to bring Jesus into the world. And in that same line is Solomon, who messed up at least as much as me.

Solomon's reputation is for wisdom, but he also sinned greatly in his later years with his hundreds of foreign wives, conspicuous wealth, and the altars he built for the gods his wives worshiped. It's always such a relief for me, although also a bit painful, to think about how fallible the people of the Bible were, even the ones God blessed greatly. God can do so much work through such limited material.

I wondered why only Joseph's lineage made the cut. Shouldn't we want to know more about Mary's family, since she was the one chosen to carry the child? If anything, Joseph seems less blessed, although it was of course a great privilege and responsibility to raise Jesus.

My sense of annoyance about Joseph only continued the next day as I read how Joseph, "a righteous man and unwilling to expose her to public disgrace, planned to dismiss her quietly" when he found out Mary was pregnant (Matthew 1:19 NRSV). He was preparing to marry her, so presumably he and his family thought she was a respectable Jewish girl. Wouldn't he have assumed she was raped? And then he would have left her to raise this child on her own with no husband to assume parentage? Wouldn't that have left her the worst kind of outcast? Or did he assume the real father would step in? These questions are, of course, left unanswered in the text.

Of course, it would be a shock to anyone to find that your fiancée was expecting a child by someone else, but still . . . poor Mary. And there is no story here of her being told that she was pregnant by the Holy Spirit. Instead, we are told that "she was found to be with child from the Holy Spirit" (Matthew 1:18 NRSV). Found by whom? And how did they know? It felt like only Joseph counted here, perhaps another function of that genealogy. I missed the part in Luke where we get her reaction to the news.

Matthew then tells us Joseph had no relations with Mary until after Jesus was born, even after they were married, and I wondered why that little tidbit was included. Was Matthew worrying that people would think Joseph got her pregnant later and she delivered early? Despite my cynical view of Matthew's motives, I have no problem with Mary becoming pregnant by the Holy Spirit. I truly believe Jesus was God's Son, in every way that counts. I thought again of Strobel's talk; he was so careful to say that everything logical in the Scriptures pointed to Jesus' dying and being physically resurrected. He said that the facts were like a rushing current that overwhelmed him with their truth. As much as I appreciate and even take strength from conversion stories like his, I still find myself thinking, *What about faith?*

I feel that we're not supposed to know beyond a shadow of a doubt, and that Jesus himself really was a bit cagey about the whole thing by describing himself as the Son of Man. I like having to bridge the gap a bit, so to speak, with faith. The idea that it is all logical, and only an idiot would deny the facts, is not so appealing to me. At the

---

What Works for Me

Shelly, pastor and mother of three

I am an early riser, and I find that before dawn is my time. That's where I can pull the Bible out and read. I think it's difficult to read for the joy of the Scripture instead of for the work that you have to do, so the way I find it is before the world awakens, in the darkness of the morning before the birds begin to sing. I find that once people are up and the work of the day begins that I'm about the work of the day, but if I can do it before the work of the day begins, then I can be about the work of the Spirit.

same time I do think it would be terribly hard to be an atheist, although I have no practice at it. Not because it would require believing so much more than being a Christian, as Strobel says, but because it would seem to me the scariest, darkest, most fragile of existences. What would you be anchored to? Whom would you turn to in times of grief or sorrow or celebration? And these thoughts highlighted the importance of my study endeavor. If I believe, and I do, that the Bible is the foundation of faith, the best understanding we have available to us of God and how God works in the world, then how can I have a faith without continuously studying it?

Matthew records Jesus' birth in Bethlehem, although we do not know how he got there and no stable is mentioned. But here are the wise men, sent as spies by King Herod, who is threatened by their talk of the baby as King of the Jews. (How did I forget that Herod had sent them? Probably because it is not highlighted in Christmas pageants.) But they don't return to Herod to betray Jesus' whereabouts; a dream warns them not to. All these dreams! Joseph receives three dreams—one about the baby to be born, two about where it is safe to take his family. I wasn't supposed to be focusing on life application in my study plan, but I couldn't help but wonder here if God ever spoke to me in dreams. I didn't even remember my dreams very often anymore. And how could I have forgotten about Herod killing all the babies two and under in Bethlehem? This time as I read it, a cold finger ran down my spine. *That would have been Ben.*

John the Baptist also comes across scarier than I remembered him. I have a leftover-from-Sunday-school image of John the Baptist as a harmless but weird desert loner, wearing his scratchy camel-hair clothes and eating bugs. But when the Pharisees and Sadducees come to the Jordan River to be baptized by him, I am struck by the threatening tone he takes with them, calling them a "brood of vipers," questioning their very identity as descendants of Abraham, and going on about baptism by fire. When Jesus finally comes to John and John tells Jesus that Jesus should baptize him, I find myself in agreement. It certainly seems more logical for Jesus to baptize John than the other way around. The footnote in my Bible tells me it is necessary for Jesus to be anointed as the "righteous king." I am also struck by the complete unambiguity of the voice from heaven calling Jesus his beloved Son. I had been thinking of Jesus as being perhaps a bit mysterious by describing himself as the ambiguous "Son of Man," but the voices in the Bible around him were not cagey or subtle in the least.

"Give to Everyone . . ."

It was now Holy Week in the world, although I had not quite caught up to the world in my Bible reading. We attended a dinner and Passover tableau at our new church on Maundy Thursday. At the tableau, members of the congregation dressed as Jesus and his disciples, and I found myself transfixed as they enacted the scene at the table (as shown in da Vinci's *The Last Supper* painting). Reacquainting myself with Jesus as I had been doing in Matthew made his death, the loss his disciples must have felt, seem more real, more personal.

On Easter morning, we got up and walked to church in the sunshine, where we sang my favorite hymn, "Christ the Lord Is Risen Today." The Resurrection, too, seemed more joyful this year, which made sense. When your lows are low, your highs feel higher. If anything, motherhood had taught me that. We celebrated with a train-themed Easter basket for Ben and an Easter egg hunt and chocolate French toast with friends. Then a three-hour nap for all.

The next morning I read the Sermon on the Mount, which I love. I was tempted to sit and spend some time on the various sayings, but instead tried to keep moving through, reminding myself that this was not the month for meditative reading. I floated through a lot of familiar passages in the Sermon until I reached "Give to everyone who begs from you, and do not refuse anyone who wants to borrow from you." Here I had to stop, despite my "study" focus. This teaching about how we are to treat those who ask something from us has always troubled me.

When I lived in Berkeley, California, I would pass by dozens of homeless people on a daily basis on my way to and from work in a downtown San Francisco office building. Often I would buy a dollar bagel for breakfast and then give a dollar or any change I had to a guy who sat right outside the building. I never gave to "everyone," but I tried to give when I could and not to be too judgey about it, which was tough for me. I seem to be gifted at judgment.

Still, I have always been troubled by what to do when approached by a panhandler. There was one woman in particular who had straw-like blonde hair and the weather-scarred face that I had learned to recognize as a sign that she probably did, in fact, sleep outdoors. She would approach people rapidly outside the North Berkeley BART station and say things like, "Give me some money," in her deep, raspy voice. It made me feel like a bank she was trying to rob. I never gave her any. She seemed threatening, and, well, she didn't ask nicely!

Periodically, I would ask myself if she was Jesus. You know, the Jesus of a later passage in Matthew, 25:31-46, where he commends those who clothed, fed, and cared for others, saying that it was he himself they cared for; and condemns those who failed to care for others, saying again that it was Jesus himself for whom they failed to care. Was that lady Jesus? The thought gave me pause, but I still never gave her any money.

Although I no longer walk a daily gauntlet of panhandlers, in our area panhandlers frequent local stoplights and medians, holding signs asking for money. I never give them any money either. I'm afraid to roll down my window and get out my purse. I occasionally think that I should make kits in my car with water bottles and granola bars and a dollar bill, but I've never done it. Are these more Jesuses that I am failing?

Yet that whole judginess sneaks back in. As an undergraduate student in a study-abroad program in London, I always passed by one woman who sat in a doorway right outside the neighborhood grocery store asking for money. She often had a child or two huddled with her. I often gave her my change, and one day I bought an extra loaf of bread and handed that to her instead. She gave me one of the ugliest looks I had ever seen before or since. If the idea of a loaf of bread was so disgusting to her, what was she using my money for? Perhaps the children were gluten-free, but I never gave her money (or bread) again, feeling like I knew her game.

Are such reactions appropriate? Are we to give to everyone and not ask what the money is for, or how deserving they are?

Part of my focus on study this month involved looking at each passage in context, and so I noticed that Jesus makes this comment about giving to "everyone who asks" right after he advises that we turn the other cheek, give a cloak to anyone who asks for our coat, and walk a second mile for anyone who forces you to go one. In light of these statements, I wondered if there was perhaps a little exaggeration here for effect and whether these statements were not necessarily meant to be literal instructions for life. Or maybe I didn't want them to be.

Reading by Myself?

All this internal wrestling over one little line of Scripture! It brought up another question: How exactly are we meant to make Scripture part of our lives? We place such a heavy emphasis today on individual time alone with the Bible, which is a relatively recent idea in church history. Yet, in *Velvet Elvis*, Rob Bell points out that nobody ever read the Bible alone in Jesus' time. They had no printing presses—copies of Scripture were few and far between, so Scripture reading and study were done only as a community. Group study was not only practical, it was also helpful as a corrective. The combination of everyone's experiences and perspectives and knowledge helped keep any one person from going too far off the rails in their interpretation. Reading in community helped keep everyone in balance.

I had never before considered that individual Bible study might not be adequate, but when I reflected on it, I wondered if that was one reason I have always enjoyed Bible study groups, and why group study seems to come more easily and often be more fulfilling than reading the Bible on my own, even for someone as introverted as me.

I continued through the words of the Sermon on the Mount, pausing to reflect briefly on favorite verses about praying for those who persecute you and not worrying about our lives because of the way God cares for the birds and the lilies. One verse in particular had recently become even more meaningful: if we, evil as we are, give our children what they ask for, then what more does God do for us? But this question about individual study became a constant hum in the back of my head. As much as I was a loner who hated working in teams (sad but true), I still didn't do all that well at Bible study by myself. I truly enjoyed the Bible in all its diversity, trying to put pieces together, see links, and reach new understanding, but I really did those things well only when I was doing them in community with others. That was why I liked taking religion classes in the first place.

Along with concluding that I needed to add some sort of group component to my study practice in the future, I was also realizing just how far I was from my study goal. At this late date, I realized I should have made a study plan instead of just leaving my Bible open on my desk and reading when I took a work break here and there. As a life-long procrastinator and crammer, normally I would have responded to the approaching deadline by speed-reading or pulling a late night.

But that wasn't the point here, was it? So instead I stopped trying to push myself to go faster and just let myself read what I read. Just when I was starting to wonder if I would ever get through the Sermon on the Mount, Jesus came down from the mountain and started to heal. I was fascinated by Jesus telling the Roman centurion that he had not found such faith in anyone in Israel. Ouch, that must have stung the disciples. And in the very next story is a quotation from Isaiah about Jesus taking on our infirmities and bearing our diseases. I had never really paid much attention to this idea of healing as causing Jesus to suffer outside the cross. It seemed to me to have so many ramifications. Is this true for all who heal through their prayers? Or does Jesus take on these sicknesses, too, even as he can heal through our prayers? Should I be more cautious in asking for healing when considering that Jesus literally takes on the sickness? Or was all his taking on of our infirmities completed forever and in perpetuity when he died on the cross? My inclination was to answer yes, but I felt again how much I would have loved to discuss these thoughts with others, and how much depth, perspective, and perhaps even correction that would bring to my study.

I was saddened by Jesus' statements about having nowhere to lay his head. And then he refused to let a disciple go bury his own father. Another troublesome teaching. I feel confident that I can trust in Jesus more perfectly than I can even trust in my own family, but to turn my back on my family? Could I do that? Would Jesus ask it of me?

I moved through the stories of his ministry and that of the disciples, still finding many new things to ponder. Why do I never remember that girl he raised from the dead, but instead remember only the woman who touched his cloak in the same chapter? And I noticed so much foreshadowing of trouble, for example, Jesus' ominous words to the disciples as he sends them out on their own (how can they possibly be ready? will they ever be? will I ever be?). The people will turn against them, Jesus warns. They will be persecuted, he tells them. And of course, they are. The story was coming alive for me now, the reading coming more quickly. Yet as the month came to a close, I had barely reached the middle of Matthew, far short of my goal of finishing all four Gospels and Romans.

I was not as disappointed about this as I might have thought. What stood out about my month of studying Matthew was how many surprises there were in a story I thought was entirely familiar. I could no longer excuse myself from Bible reading on the grounds that I already knew a lot of it because, obviously, even a book I thought I knew well still held much to ponder and learn. If I'd speed-read through all the Gospels as I'd planned, surely I would have missed a lot of those little things. I couldn't approach the Bible as I did a lot of my reading—speeding through like the book could self-combust at any moment. And rushing through in order to conquer, get through, get done was my MO in more things than just reading. You don't get to conquer parenting. And no matter how many books you read, there is no guarantee of success. What exactly is success when it comes to parenting, anyway?

Maybe I had been right with my initial instinct at the beginning of the month—that what I needed was a more meditative look at brief Scripture passages. But then I wouldn't have experienced the larger story, the all-important context.

It seemed to me at least a possibility that this month I had studied exactly the quantity God wanted me to.

Non-Expert Tips for Practicing Study

1. Remember that the reading is for you, a free gift from God. Remind yourself of this truth especially when you forget to study.

2. The Bible is the story of how God has been and is with us, with all the attendant complexity and nuance. It is not helpful to read it like you're cramming for a midterm.

3. Don't set such high expectations of your Bible study that you cannot possibly succeed. Focus less on pages read and books completed than on understandings given and insights gained. Pay attention to the Holy Spirit telling you when you need to slow down and reflect. Sometimes less is more.

4. Find a community to help you learn—to keep you going and to keep you balanced.

5. Let God be in charge.

5

SIMPLICITY: TAKING IT ONE THING AT A TIME

May

Simplicity is freedom.
—Richard J. Foster, *Celebration of Discipline*

The thought of practicing simplicity evoked an image of a perfectly organized, minimalist home with white walls and a tidy linen closet and all the toys relegated to labeled bins in the children's room. That is, if kids were allowed. In fact, just the word *simplicity* filled me with a sense of longing and inadequacy, since this minimalist home was not, unfortunately, my reality. My home was a place where clean sheets and towels were grabbed straight from the laundry basket, plastic toys were strewn all over the family room floor, and dust bunnies were our loyal pets, but that didn't stop me from wishing for that ideal.

This desire ran deep in me. I reached adulthood with Martha Stewart on TV and *Real Simple* magazines on the shelves. I loved The Container Store, even though, as my aunt once pointed out, it is just a store full of boxes. Deep down I thought that my home was supposed to resemble the cover of an interior design magazine, and I also suspected that if it did, my life and the lives of everyone in my family would be better.

My other idea of simplicity involved spending no money. Frankly, that didn't appeal to me as much. So when I started thinking about practicing simplicity as a spiritual discipline, I approached it with a dual sense of enthusiasm and reluctance. On the one hand, I was ready to get my house into shape; but on the other hand, I wasn't sure I was ready to give up Target.

As I discovered, biblical simplicity is a lot less about organizing our possessions than it is about being free of them. *The Life with God Bible* defines *simplicity* as "the inward reality of single-hearted focus upon God and his kingdom, which results in an outward lifestyle of modesty, openness, and unpretentiousness and which disciplines our hunger for status, glamour, and luxury." Suffice it to say, it's quite different from my initial ideas. In biblical simplicity we start with a focus on God, and the *result* is changes in our outward lifestyle. Simplicity is not about the way things look but about the way we *are*, the way we think.

Indeed, the idea of simplicity itself can become an idol—an idol with its own practices (give one piece of clothing away for every piece you buy!) and texts (organized living magazines). I realized that where I had gone wrong with my preconceived notions of simplicity was focusing on the result—the outward lifestyle, rather than the cause—focusing on God. So I began my attempt to practice simplicity by seeking to cultivate three inward attitudes described in *Celebration of Discipline*: knowing that what we have is a gift from God, feeling a lack of anxiety about our things (i.e., trusting God with them), and allowing our possessions to be available to all others. Of these three, the idea of trying not to be anxious about our things seemed easiest. Having a child had already helped me tremendously with this concept. After your baby spits up or spills on you most days, or your toddler pulls the pages out of your books and gets fingerprints on every surface he can reach, you start to hold on to your possessions a little more lightly. After all, when it comes down to child or stuff, for most of us it's not a tough choice.

But I could definitely work on the other two attitudes, knowing what I had was a gift from God and making my possessions available to others. Unlike some of the other disciplines I'd tried, simplicity didn't seem to be one I could practice each day for twenty minutes, although probably I could have found some value in doing that. Instead, I tried to follow some general principles. In keeping with Foster's first inward attitude, the idea of thinking of all I had as a gift from God, I tried to appreciate what I already had and not acquire new stuff.

Out with the New

Each day when the mail came, I walked straight to the recycling bin and threw out every catalog without looking at it. I was tempted to peek only a couple of times. For the most part, getting rid of all the kids, clothing, and home decor catalogs was a huge relief. Not only did those catalogs tempt me to buy new things, they tended to stack up on my counters, waiting for me either to flip through them or to decide if I still wanted to buy something on a page I'd dog-eared.

Reducing the catalog pile on my countertop helped me see that my hoarder tendencies ramped into overdrive when it came to reading material. Newspapers, magazines, newsletters, school announcements—they piled up like crazy, and I had a terrible time reducing the piles because I wanted to read all of the stuff and didn't ever seem to have time. So I also started to throw out my newspaper at the end of each day whether I'd read it or not. (I had a harder time with the magazines, but, hey, baby steps.) Just recycling the catalogs and newspapers went a long way toward reducing my counter clutter and freed up some extra time as well.

I also worked on going through my clothes with an eye toward giving some away, and although I was hampered by a desire to try on every single item before making a decision, I did move a lot of stuff to the giveaway pile in the garage.

Even though I wasn't indulging in any catalog lust, it was tough not to spend money on anything we didn't *need*. It helped that I knew it was only a temporary commitment so I could just tell myself I was putting off purchases for a month. One thing was immediately clear: I had to avoid Target. Target stores cast some kind of buying spell on me. Even when I walked in just to buy a birthday card, I always emerged with an entire shopping cart full of stuff. And since I hadn't intended to buy any of it, I couldn't avoid the conclusion that the vast majority of these purchases was stuff I didn't need, as appealing as that rubber frog/Lego set/decorative basket/book/flowered file folder may be.

Free Time

In addition to avoiding catalogs, online shopping, and certain stores (we still had to get groceries, of course), I tried to limit our activities to things that were already free and available, like our back-yard and the local parks. Ben and I spent a lot of time hanging out in our backyard, which was actually pretty fun. One of the best things about living in Southern California is that you can grow just about anything, and, thankfully, the person who'd lived in our house before us had planted lots of stuff. We checked out the oranges and plums and monitored the progress of the tomatoes, blueberries, and grapes. Some of these plants didn't look like they were doing too well, but we didn't really know what they were supposed to look like, so we hoped for the best and watered everything for good measure. And we kicked the soccer ball around. A lot. There wasn't much Ben liked to do more than kick the soccer ball around, but eventually even he got a little cabin fever. I knew it was time to hit the park.

So here's my deep dark maternal secret: I've never really liked going to the park. I know it's supposed to be every mother's favorite activity, but I found it, well, "boring" would be an understatement. I had to make sure Ben was playing nice with the other kids, and that we both had enough sunscreen on, and that we had adequate supplies of water and snacks and any other sundries Ben might request. It just seemed like a lot of work. When I did manage to organize a park outing, I felt exhausted in a kind of victorious way afterward, like I needed a cupcake reward.

But at this point we'd played at home for days, so I thought I'd take him to a nearby park we'd often driven by. I had thought many times that we should go there. You know, one day. I had even tried a couple of times to walk there with Ben in the stroller, but it was on a busy road without a sidewalk and I could never find a way to walk there safely. So we'd always had to turn around, to Ben's great regret if not my own. I had finally figured out a back way to walk there on streets with sidewalks. So we set out with the jogging stroller—exercise plus stimulating but free park activity. It was sad to realize that even in my simplicity practice I was still trying to two-for-one. It was about a twenty-minute walk, and by the time we got there, Ben was more than ready to jump out of the stroller and play.

At first glance, the park didn't look like much to me. It was really more of a playground maintained by a local church on the edge of their property. It was weedy and dark, with a lot of scraggly trees, and the play structures, with their peeling paint, didn't look all that safe. Or fun. But what did I know? I'd long been aware that the things I thought Ben would like—say, clean and fully functioning toys—were often not the things he actually played with. He loved the gym kids club that I hated because it always looked dirty. But it was filled with lots of other kids, and they had two beach balls that they let him kick into the Pack 'n Plays (heaven help us if they ever try to put a baby in there) and a large tackle box filled with broken-off bits of crayon that he could use to color the copies they made of pages from Disney coloring books. That was enough for him.

And it was the same thing with the park. He loved the weeds and trees because they attracted lots of birds for him to look at. And he certainly didn't care that the playground toys were old and peeling paint. All he cared about was whether he could play on them and how many friends were there to join him. And if the swings worked. Ben could swing all day. It was not all that unusual for me to have to drag him out of a swing and straight to the stroller or car, kicking and screaming. (Come to think of it, perhaps that was one of the reasons I disliked the park.) As I pushed him on the swing and he cackled with delight, I thought about which of us was better at practicing simplicity. It was pretty obvious it wasn't me. So I climbed on the swing next to Ben and for once I tried to power off the to-do list. At least until he was ready to go. I, too, used to think swinging was the greatest thing in the world. Turned out it was still pretty fun.

When he started yawning, he let me strap him into the stroller, and we walked home. At one point walking, at least as a method of traveling from one destination to another, had been foreign to me. Where I grew up, in a suburban neighborhood in southern Illinois, you might walk the dog around the block, but you didn't walk somewhere for an errand. When I moved to Northern California for grad school with two suitcases and no car, however, I quickly learned to walk everywhere—to school, to the grocery store (where I limited myself severely as to the weight of the groceries that I would have to carry up the hill and home—absolutely no cans of soup!), to the Laundromat, to the gym, to church. I eventually got a bus pass, which was a good thing because I could buy a larger variety of groceries (and also because I met my husband riding the bus), but I never got over my love of walking. So when we moved to Southern California, we made sure to find a home where we could walk to church, the library, and the grocery store. Statistically it seemed safer to avoid driving when we could, and both Ben and I liked to be out in the air. I often thought that if I hadn't been living somewhere I could walk outside every day when I first had Ben, I would have lost my mind.

What Works for Me

Sara, tack shop owner and mom of one

With a small house, I can't keep everything so we make a lot of donations, even toys and things that my daughter still plays with. She has to make everything fit in a basket, and whatever doesn't fit, we donate. She gets to pick. If something's really important, she has to put that in first. I think it teaches her that sometimes you have to do things for other people by giving stuff away to kids who don't have as many things. It is sacrifice on a very small level, but to a six-year-old, giving away a teddy bear is a big deal, so we talk about it as giving it up for the joy of another person, so they can share in your wealth. Every time we give something away, we pray over it, that the recipient will love it and be blessed.

Because we did walk so much, we had only one car. Usually it stayed home with me, and my husband biked or took the bus to work, but some days he needed the car for work. Too often on those days I remembered my lack of a vehicle with a sense of annoyance, frequently while I was walking out the door with keys in hand. I'd have to turn to Ben with a *Well, looks like we won't be doing* that *today* grimace.

Focusing on simplicity, though, changed the way I thought about not having a car. The limitations it sometimes forced on us began to seem more like a gift. When we didn't have that car ready to go, our choices were a lot fewer. We had to find sometfhing to do at home or go somewhere within walking distance. We didn't even have to consider SeaWorld or Costco or the mom's café or the gymnastics place or the shopping mall.

A parenting coach in a class I'd taken had advised us to offer our kids options, but not too many. Three was good, two better. It seemed the same principle was true for me. It was so much easier to figure out what we were going to do when our choices were limited. Too often in life we have such a dizzying array of options available to us that choosing can be overwhelming and stressful. Just ask someone from another country what he or she thinks of the average American cereal aisle. To my surprise, I found consciously limiting my options to be . . . relaxing, of all things.

As the summer approached, I tried to think about how I might continue to exercise this idea of limiting our options. I didn't think Ben was an overscheduled child. He had preschool three mornings a week and then sports class one afternoon a week, but the looming summer had me wondering what I was going to do with him at home all day every day. I asked one of his teachers if there were any summer camps or activities that she recommended for a child Ben's age, and she frowned at me. "Just enjoy him!" she said. "This time will go so fast."

I groaned inwardly. It was a helpful reminder, but still. . . . It seemed to me that her response was one of the constant refrains of motherhood. Older women would stop us in the grocery store, lean over, and advise, "Just enjoy it. This time goes so fast. Just you wait!" It was hard to know how to respond, except with more guilt. I had no doubt this was true. After all, time was already playing funny games with my memory. Although it seemed like three seconds had passed since Ben had been a newborn, at the same time I couldn't remember life without him. And yet, how exactly was "enjoying him" supposed to work? Did it mean never being apart from him? I felt like the occasional activity for him or babysitting time helped me value my time with him even more. His teacher's words made me doubt myself. Was I just making excuses? Where was the balance for me in spending time with him and having time for myself? I didn't have any easy answers to that.

Giving Freely

Of Foster's three suggestions, I found the last one, the idea of allowing our possessions to be available to all others, to be the most difficult. I have a friend who is so giving with her possessions that if I admire something of hers, she will more than likely give it to me. It turned out I was not so giving. For example, one of Ben's preschool teachers asked if she could have a little yellow shirt of his printed with a soccer ball and the number five when he outgrew it. She wanted to use it in a T-shirt quilt for her daughter, whose high school soccer number had been five. "Oh, sure!" I said automatically.

But I realized I really didn't want to give her the shirt.

My thoughts ran along these lines: *Oh, but Ben likes soccer so much, and he looks so cute in that color, and the shirt has matching pants, and he won't outgrow it by the time she needs it to make that quilt. Plus, we plan to have another child and what if we have a boy and then won't I want him to have that shirt?*

Talk about a hoarding mentality.

Ben had plenty of shirts. However much I liked that particular one, what she wanted it for was special, and she was a lovely person who'd loved and cared for my son. Plus, I couldn't deny that it was a clear opportunity to practice simplicity. So I gave her the shirt, even though I still felt a little grudging about it. But of course, it felt really good to be able to do something nice for this woman who'd done so much for us. Sometimes in the spiritual life, at least in my spiritual life, I find I have to force myself to act even when my heart is not fully on board. More often than not, the result shames me into being a little more giving and open the next time around.

The Best Teacher

My efforts aside, I learned the most about simplicity from Ben. Simplicity was effortless for him. He could be entertained for hours by a bug. He was completely satisfied with a book, or a box, or a pile of weeds. Me, not so much. After a few minutes of playing soccer with him in the backyard, I would feel a burning need to water the plants or throw a load in the washer or gather plums or clean something. I was always telling him, "Just a minute. Let me just do this one thing, then I'll be right with you." Of course, it was never just a minute. I was teaching him that he didn't deserve my full attention. In contrast, he almost always offered me his. He didn't have to have the TV on, or be reading something, or doing twelve things at once to be content.

His example helped me realize that perhaps the biggest obstacle to simplicity in my life was my focus on multitasking, something I'd always felt was a strength. Multitasking, of course, is something we all do—women are particularly good at it, and it's often necessary to make our lives work—but there are times when multitasking is not appropriate.

All those little tasks I was always doing were taking my time and focus away from my son, and I saw clearly how they were also taking my time and focus away from God. Both deserved my undivided attention.

I realized I'd come full circle—back to the idea of simplicity as a full-hearted focus on God. The key to the whole thing was paying attention to what was taking away from my inward focus on God. Sometimes it was spending money and acquiring stuff. I noticed at the end of the month that the purchases I had "put off" seemed a lot less urgent. Somehow an enforced waiting period helped foster within me a little spending resistance.

Sometimes it was clutter that was distracting me, so throwing away all the catalogs was definitely a practice to keep. Other times it was TV, radio, or even the books or newspapers I was reading. Sometimes it was just the to-do list that runs nonstop through my mind. Turning it off or trying to do a little less of whatever I felt was taking me away from God seemed to help, but there were still decisions that weren't so easy. I could try to reduce the demands of my life, but there would always be some demands. And figuring out the balance was always going to be hard. Was Ben doing too much or too little? Was I "enjoying" him the proper amount? Like so much in my life, it seemed those things were going to have to be decided on a case-by-case basis.

One of the best lessons motherhood had taught me was that it's okay, even preferable, to have long periods of unscheduled time. Yet it was still a struggle for me—should Ben be in gymnastics, piano lessons, or karate? Why hadn't I taught him Spanish yet? Breathe, Julia.

It came down to this. So my e-mail was still a black hole with 3,476 unread messages, and there were currently three full laundry baskets taking up way too much floor space, but I just read a story to my child, and that was going to have to be good enough for today.

Non-Expert Tips for Practicing Simplicity

1. Open your mail over the recycling bin. Throw in all the catalogs. Remember: if you really need it (whatever "it" is), you can always specifically look it up or find it in a store.

2. Try to spend a whole day not multitasking. If that seems too hard, then just try it for an hour.

3. When you start thinking about what you do not have or what you want, try to fix your thoughts on what you already have. Pray for contentment.

4. Spend an hour doing exactly what your child wants to do. Okay, if you're like me, start with twenty minutes.

5. For one week, try to say no to every other request that is not directly work- or family-related.

6
SILENCE: TURNING IT ALL OFF

June

The eternal silence of the infinite spaces terrifies me.
—Blaise Pascal

The contemplative prayer practice I'd started in January continued to illuminate the stark contrast between those moments of silence and the rest of my life. Between Ben and his noisy toys and music and the TV and our dog and the neighbors' dogs and car horns and planes overhead, I had almost no quiet in my life. And how was I supposed to get it? Silence was another discipline that seemed almost laughable for a mom with a small child. Yes, I would love to have more silence, but I would have to pay someone to provide it for me.

At least that was how I felt when I first started to think about silence. *The Life with God Bible* defines the spiritual practice of silence in a broader way, however, as "closing off our souls from 'sounds,' whether noise, music, or words, so that we may better still the inner chatter and clatter of our noisy hearts and be increasingly attentive to God." Silence by this perspective wasn't so much about being alone in a quiet place but about learning to create an inner silence even in the midst of outside noise. It was about a silence of the soul, as described in Psalm 62:5: "For God alone my soul waits in silence, / for my hope is from him" (NRSV).

And when I started to pay attention, I realized the noise in my life was not, as I had assumed, forced upon me by Ben and others. Rather, I was the one introducing a lot of the sound into our day by turning on the radio or playlist or TV. Was I afraid of being bored? Afraid of being alone with my own thoughts? Dallas Willard writes,

> Silence is frightening because it strips us as nothing else does, throwing us upon the stark realities of our life. It reminds us of death, which will cut us off from this world and leave only us and God. And in that quiet, what if there turns out to be very little to "just us and God"? Think what it says about the inward emptiness of our lives if we must *always* turn on the tape player or the radio to make sure something is happening around us.

That hit home. As much as I'd thought I wanted silence, the reality of it was daunting.

Last month I'd thought quite a bit about my multitasking obsession and how it carried over to media. I was often reading the paper *and* listening to the radio or writing with music or TV on in the background. And it wasn't just sound that was the problem. Even those silent forms of media were noisy, in that they filled my head with stuff, sometimes interesting and beautiful things, but more often problems and anxieties. When I was preparing a meal—a prime opportunity to talk to Ben—I often had a newspaper or a magazine or a book, or all three, with me there in the kitchen. I would take little hits of reading material between conversational gambits, like an alcoholic sneaking drinks.

And this media noise was not relaxing, most of the time. The magazines and newspapers in particular often stressed me out—SO MUCH to learn about the world, SO MANY new parenting techniques and healthy recipes to try or file away. There was a lot of noise around, and I was welcoming it in.

This was nothing new for me, frankly. I remember doing my high school math homework on the couch while I was watching TV with my family. It seemed a lot more fun than working on it by myself in my room. And when I was in college, I was infamous for watching whackadoodle Lifetime movies in the wee hours while I was writing papers. When I moved to Berkeley for grad school and lived by myself for the first time, I had the TV on almost all the time. I liked the noise, the company. I could write with it on, read with it on—basically the only thing I did without the TV on was study Greek. I needed all my faculties for that.

Maybe all this television was why I felt so scattered all the time. Had I eroded my ability to concentrate? I hoped that seeking more silence might help me continue with my practice of simplicity, of focusing on one thing at a time.

Radio Silence

I'd established that I was not particularly great at silence. My goals for the month were to have more times of silence, and to listen more and talk less, as I'd tried when practicing fellowship and submission. Although there are many beautiful Bible verses about seeking God in silence, the one I found most motivating for my practice was James 1:19: "Know this, my dear brothers and sisters: everyone should be quick to listen, slow to speak, and slow to grow angry."

Silence is meant to be a stress reliever, and I could understand why. Aren't there times when there's so much going on that you just think your head is going to explode? And then you turn off the TV or the radio and just want to say "Aaahhhh . . ." It makes you wonder why you turned it on in the first place. I'd read that driving without the radio or any music on could be a tremendous stress reliever, so I started doing that for the short drives I took on my own a few miles up the street to write or edit at a local Peet's Coffee & Tea.

I was skeptical at first of the possible effects of such a small change, but it worked immediately. When I drove in silence, I found my thoughts turned to God. It took only the few minutes of driving time that I had to make me feel more peaceful, plus, I reached my destination in a far better, calmer mood. I only wished I'd made this discovery earlier.

The other aspect of silence I wanted to work on was listening more and talking less, particularly at home. I had noticed that I always turned on the radio or my iPod in the kitchen when I was making breakfast for Ben or we were having lunch together. I actually felt kind of uncomfortable with the idea of just sitting and having a conversation with Ben without the radio or anything in the background.

Just that realization was enough to convince me that I absolutely had to do just that—be intentional about conversation with Ben, *without* background noise.

Ben and I had come a long way since my early days of trying to fill his days with a certain number of words. He had learned to talk fairly early, to my great relief, since there's nothing more frustrating than a crying child who cannot tell you what he wants or needs and also because I wasn't with-it enough to teach him sign language. That seemed to be the province of those really advanced mothers. (I had come to the conclusion that you could do certain things but not everything. For example, I could make his food from scratch but then I didn't manage to scrub the bathtub or mop the floor. He got to go on lots of walks and had many, many books read to him, but no sign language or Spanish. I am a lot more blasé about this now than I was then.) But the fact that he could talk didn't necessarily mean we had the most scintillating conversations. Here's how an average conversation of ours went:

Me (in bright mommy voice): What do you want to do today?
Ben: Let's play soccer.
Me: OK.
Ben: Want to play soccer now.
Me: We're eating lunch now. But we can play after your nap.
Ben: Want to play soccer *now*.
Me: We're eating lunch now. But we can play after your nap.
Ben: I don't want to nap. I want to play soccer!

But we talked, and I worked on listening and focusing only on him. Paying attention was both harder and easier than I had thought. Harder to get started—I realized the radio performed the important function of easing me into a conversational place—but so much more fun once we got going. And I found that we more often did go do the fun stuff he wanted after our meal when I spent it focused on him and not getting pulled in ten different directions by the radio or the phone or the book or whatever else I was sharing focus with.

When it came to silence and every other spiritual practice, I was starting to realize that one of the most effective things I could do was just to pay attention.

A Sort-of Silent Retreat, Interrupted

I was at a place with work where I had no copyedits or drafts due; my main project was preparing a talk about practicing spiritual disciplines for a Renovaré conference later in the month. One of the reasons I'd picked silence that month was that I knew I'd be going to the retreat all by my lonesome, and I was beyond excited. Ever since having Ben, I found myself daydreaming (and night dreaming too) about sleeping alone in a big, beautiful hotel bed with clean white sheets. Sleeping all night, with no interruptions. This conference was going to be my chance to do that. I had a room all to myself; it was as close as I was going to get for some time to a silent retreat.

Then, a week before I was to fly to San Antonio for the conference, we had a party at our house, and one of Ryan's colleagues brought a shrimp appetizer with some fresh dill as a garnish. Although I'd never been particularly bothered by the smell of dill before, that night I could not even be in the same room with it.

As soon as the party was over, I threw out the rest of the dill and took out the kitchen trash to get rid of the smell. Even so, the next morning I could still smell it in the kitchen. A little warning bell started going off in my head. When was the last time I'd been so sensitive to smells?

Ryan and I had been hoping to have another baby, but unlike last time, when I'd gotten pregnant just about as the thought crossed my mind, this time it had been a few months. I had taken a test just a week earlier and it had been negative, but perhaps I had taken it too early. I didn't want to say anything to Ryan, to get his hopes up without cause, so I took another test while he was at work. As usual, Ben was in the bathroom with me, so he watched curiously as I stared at the two pink lines that immediately showed up. I was shocked but happy. Jump-up-and-down-and-swing-Ben-around happy.

I wanted to tell Ryan right away, but unfortunately when I called him he had just watched the U.S. men's soccer team lose a game on his lunch break, so I decided to hold off. That night he was coming home with a good friend of ours who was joining us for dinner. Inspired by my silence practice, I decided to tell him without words by leaving the positive test on his side of our bathroom sink. All day I looked forward to seeing Ryan's face after he saw it, and when they finally got home, I kept waiting for him to head back there, but instead he joined me in the kitchen and helped me finish up dinner and get the table ready. I was about ready to make up something he needed to do in our bedroom when he finally went in to change his clothes. Although I'd been chomping at the bit for him to see it, now that he actually was back there, I felt nervous. I kept losing track of what our friend was saying. Would Ryan see the test? Would he know what it meant? When he came out I could hardly even meet his eyes, but he came directly to me with a huge grin and gave me a furtive hug. "Wow!" he whispered in my ear. Now it was our secret.

That had been so much more fun than actually saying the words.

What Works for Me

Carrie, former attorney, writer, and mother of two children and two furry nightmares

Despite having two boys and two yappy dogs, I believe social media is the noisiest part of my day, particularly when reading rants on controversial subjects. Sometimes figurative noise blares so loud I can't hear the harmony of my own thoughts. I try to limit my social media intake both in duration and scope, and by doing so regain valuable time, affinity with family, and solace.

Being pregnant gave me a new take on silence. I was thrilled but didn't want to announce anything until I was a little further along, so I kept the news to myself as we went through the week. Inside, though, I was quietly ecstatic, giving God high-fives in my head.

My joy about the pregnancy added to my anticipation of the conference, my Big Silence Experience. But when the morning I was to fly out arrived, I found myself so doubled over with morning sickness I couldn't even make my flight. I spent most of the morning on the bathroom floor and managed to make it onto a later flight. By the time I arrived at the hotel that night, I felt more or less human. But the next morning before my talk, I woke feeling even worse than the previous day. How was I going to even make it to the talk, much less give it?

Yes, it was ironic. Here it was—my long-anticipated silence, and I was too sick and worried to enjoy it.

Forty-five minutes before my scheduled talk, I dragged myself out of bed and started to walk to the Baptist church where I was to give my talk. It wasn't far—maybe half a mile, but I was walking at the pace of a ninety-year-old woman, so it was good I started early. I moved slowly and stiffly down the street, feeling as though every new smell—gasoline fumes, cooking food, garbage—was personally assaulting me, but my snail's pace got me there.

I set up my folder on the podium and was shocked to see that people were already starting to arrive, a full half hour before the talk was even to begin. I had been planning to, I don't know, lie down on the floor in front of the podium for a few minutes and pray for the strength to stand up for the full hour, and here people were, already ready to go. At first I was overwhelmed by another wave of panic, but the fact that I felt so bad actually cut down on my nerves. No longer was I focused on giving the greatest talk ever—now I was just hoping not to vomit into the microphone.

I started chatting with a few of the women and admitted how bad I was feeling. As is usually the case with moms, they were sympathetic and kind to a one. Later, I realized I was attempting a time-tested political strategy of debate prep—lower everyone's expectations to the point where just the fact that you stood at the front of the room for the entire allotted period was a victory.

But most important, those sweet audience members prayed for me right there in their seats. And you know what? Their prayers worked. The talk went fine, and so did the one the day after.

A Time for Silence . . . and a Time for Talking

After my two talks, the pressure was off and I was able to enjoy my semi-silent retreat, especially once the nausea-filled mornings had melted into afternoon. I kept running into people who had heard me speak. To a one, they were extremely kind and encouraging. I was so very grateful to hear that they appreciated my words and that what I said had been helpful, but at the same time I felt embarrassed by their kindness. When I kept encountering a few of the same people over and over again, I started wanting to go in the other direction so I could avoid talking to them anymore.

It would be nice to say this antisocial behavior was rooted in my efforts to practice silence, but it was mostly just my introverted self wanting to dive back into my shell. I also saw that it was about my wanting to be in control—doing what I wanted, when I wanted, and without being interrupted. It seemed clear that for me, properly honoring silence meant not just trying to talk less and listen more but also speaking (and listening too) sometimes when I would rather remain anonymous. It was a similar insight to my times in group Bible study, when I found that sometimes remaining completely silent allowed me to keep a critical, judgmental distance, rather than engaging or allowing others to respond to my ideas. Practicing the discipline of silence also meant knowing when to talk, or at least not using silence as an excuse for not interacting with others.

I did enjoy the long-anticipated silence of my room, and the space it afforded me to think about some of the insights I'd gained in my practices so far. And with a little practice, the silence wasn't nearly as daunting as it had felt before. But as much as I had longed to be alone in my own space, now that I was, I found myself missing Ben and Ryan and wanting to tell them about my day. Just a little taste of the more silent life I thought I had wanted made me appreciate my own noisy life and those with whom I shared it. This realization felt like a powerful gift from God.

I had to stop throwing up my hands and declaring that it was impossible for me to have silence or prayer or simplicity or (insert any discipline, really) at this stage in my life. Silence wasn't limited to a solo hotel room or a silent house—these perfect but extraordinary (at least for me) conditions. Silence wasn't an external blessing that would be granted to me one day when Ben had grown up or at least gone to elementary school. Turning off external sounds to the extent possible helped, but real silence was inward. It was quieting my own soul to focus on God. And that was just as possible in my own kitchen.

The single most productive way I found to practice silence? Simply the five or so minutes of complete quiet in the car. Such a small change, such a big help. It offered me the space to pray and to think, and perhaps most important, it offered a respite from the constant stream of new information that always seemed to be muscling its way into my already-crowded brain.

Along those same lines, silence, following on the heels of simplicity, was a discipline of abstinence, of trying to refrain from doing something. A practice like silence didn't take any extra time, just some attention. In general, those seemed so much easier for me to practice than those that involved adding something—prayer, fellowship, study—to my already-packed life. Maybe I needed to focus not on what I needed more of, but what I needed less of.

Non-Expert Tips for Practicing Silence

1. Look for little places in your day, like short car trips, where you can reduce the noise. Small times of silence can have an unexpectedly large calming effect on the rest of the day.

2. Pay attention to how you add noise to your day. Spend some time thinking about why and reflecting on how the music/radio/TV really makes you feel. Be cognizant, too, of the noise that has nothing to do with sound—social media, media in general, and so on.

3. Remember that practicing silence is also about measuring your words and listening more than you talk.

4. Don't sit around and wait for silence to be offered to you one day when your kids are grown, or your work is done, or you have more free time. You can create silence within yourself in any minute and at any place.

7

WORSHIP: MAKING AN APPOINTMENT WITH GOD

July

To worship God means to serve God. Basically there are two ways to do it. One way is to do things for God that God needs to have done— run errands for God, carry messages for God, fight on God's side, feed God's lambs, and so on. The other way is to do things for God that you need to do—sing songs to God, create beautiful things for God, give things up for God, tell God what's on your mind and in your heart, in general rejoice in God and make a fool of yourself for God the way lovers have always made fools of themselves for the one they love.
—Frederick Buechner, *Beyond Words*

I really like going to church. I like focusing on God, learning more about the Bible, singing praise songs (especially those select few that are in my range). I love taking Ben to the first part of the service, and I love even more sending him off to Sunday school when it's time. It is a great luxury to sit in a pew with Ryan and think about high-flown theological things rather than if I brought enough crackers or Thomas the Tank Engine books to keep Ben quiet for another few minutes. Trouble is, all too often when I go to church, I do not actually worship.

When I think of worship I think first of music, and music's capacity to forge an emotional connection to God. I also think about worship as something I do primarily at church, although I can and should do it at other times and places. But the truth is that far too frequently, when I am at church or, more commonly, when I am on my way home, I realize that I simply did not worship. I sang, I listened, I nodded, I talked with others, but I failed to truly enter into God's presence in a meaningful way, which is what worship truly is.

Here's my main stumbling block to worship: I am too arrogant. More precisely, I am the strangest mix of insecurity and superiority, two seemingly disparate qualities that in reality seem to propagate each other. Nowhere is that arrogance more on display than when it comes to theological matters. I truly believe that I understand only a small part of God (like that famous analogy of the blind men each describing a different part of the elephant and thinking his part constituted the whole). And I've certainly forgotten more than I ever learned in seminary, as my study of Matthew made clear. Yet, if I am honest, whether it's because of my job or my education or just an unfortunate aspect of my personality, I somehow am very convinced that I know a lot more than everybody else. And nothing separates me more efficiently from God than a nice neat theological critique of whatever someone else is saying about God.

Sermons are the worst. Just one little conclusion or interpretation that I'm not sure I agree with, and I'll pick it like a roast chicken for the entire rest of the service, sometimes even on the way home with Ryan. (In my defense, I get the same kind of over-analyzing after every soccer game he plays—we each have our niches, I suppose.)

In the hope of changing this, I was inspired by something our pastor wrote for the bulletin. He described how some of his friends had drastically improved their worship experience by simply thinking of their Sunday tradition as going to "worship" instead of going to church. Richard Foster offers another idea that I love: that we attend church *expecting* to meet God there.

These two ideas were my beginning goals for a worship practice. It seemed almost too easy, except that in practice it wasn't easy at all. To succeed I felt like I had to turn off my head, or at least the over-analytical part of it, and I couldn't seem to figure out how to do that. At the very first church service we attended with my new, improved intentions, our church's intern was preaching and I was so distracted by her preaching style and how it differed from our head pastor's and how the PowerPoint was working out, glitches and all, and analyzing her technique for connecting with the congregation, that I realized afterward I had yet again failed to worship.

Make a Joyful Noise?

Maybe I needed to begin with something other than the traditional church service. Later that week, our choir director was hosting an all-church Hymn Sing and Ice Cream Social. My husband suspected that this was actually a way for our choir director to finally get the entire congregation to choir practice, but offer free ice cream and my family is in. I felt a pleasant kind of anticipation as we gathered on white folding chairs in the courtyard on a beautiful summer afternoon. Maybe here was where I would have that experience of meeting God, that experience for which I was searching. Two minutes in, however, I remembered why singing in church is often not all that enjoyable or worshipful an experience for me. I have okay pitch, but my range is about seven notes, and it's low—somewhere in the alto/tenor range. More Tracy Chapman than Mariah Carey. (In middle school a teacher once picked me for the show choir but was quick to explain that her selection was based on my exemplary attendance.)

And I always have trouble picking out the alto line—I blame years of playing flute and piccolo and thus being always restricted to the melody or some trilling fluff on top—so I usually end up singing the soprano line, which I can't hit without either dropping down an octave or popping up into a falsetto. As a result I sing very softly, so much so that Ryan often makes fun of me or cocks his head at me, like, *Are you really singing over there or what?* So even when I really love the music and genuinely feel moved by the lyrics, I am still distracted by my lack of singing ability. Praise songs are easier because they seem to require less range. I know all the arguments about how traditional hymns are wonderful because they are so rich in theology, and I don't disagree, but for someone like me, singing hymns where I can't find the alto part is often an exercise in frustration and inadequacy rather than worship.

So there I was at the hymn sing, thinking about all these things and yet again not managing to worship. Ben, too, had had enough of this hymn-singing and started to climb under our chairs to visit his friend in the row behind us. I think we were both just holding out for the ice cream.

My vocal issues aside, however, maybe this inadequacy I was feeling (and not enjoying) was at the heart of my problems with worship. True worship can be awfully humbling. Unlike study, for example, which I find exhilarating at times, such as when I learn something new or understand a familiar passage in a different way, in worship there isn't something to "get." I don't even seem to become better at it with practice. In worship there is no getting around the fact that God is great and I am not, and I don't always like dwelling on that. It's not that I don't know it's true; it's just not always enjoyable to ruminate on. My lack of singing ability just seems to underline this fact.

I still had to get myself out of the picture. Evelyn Underhill explains this well in her seminal *Worship*:

> It is true that from first to last self-regarding elements are mixed with human worship; but these are no real parts of it. Not man's needs and wishes, but God's presence and incitement, first evoke it. As it rises towards purity and leaves egotistic piety behind, He becomes more and more the only Fact of existence, the one Reality; and the very meaning of Creation is seen to be an act of worship, a devoted proclamation of the splendour, the wonder, and the beauty of God. In this great *Sanctus*, all things justify their being and have their place. God alone matters, God alone Is—creation only matters because of Him.

I loved that idea. Worship should move away from me and toward God. I hadn't gotten there yet, but I wanted to.

What Works for Me

Karla, pastor and mom of one

I started a worship café service at church so I could have an opportunity to worship with my son. As a pastor, I'm up front a lot so by creating an informal atmosphere, we could worship together. I feel the freedom there to dance with my son, to play in the midst of worship. It's all senses, and that's how a child learns. I feel a more holistic, a more full connection with God when I'm holding my son in worship.

Worship at Home

Maybe my problem was that I had trouble entering into worship in a larger setting. Church gatherings can be distracting—it's easy to get caught up in what my friends are wearing and wondering if that was a new person over there and trying to remember if I had RSVP'd to the women's dinner.

Maybe what I needed more of was private moments of worship at home. At home I could sing the praise songs I liked and start them in whatever key I wanted. Ben, bless him, had recently told me he loved my singing voice. My heart swelled with love for him and concern for his musical future. I started reimagining as worship the moments before naptime and bedtime when I was attempting to quiet him for bed. This, I believe, was good for both of us. I sang and we prayed together. Sometimes I lost myself in prayer as Ben slept, and sometimes we both lay down and fell asleep in his toddler bed. (Props to IKEA for stability there, as I was getting heavier by the minute.)

In the past I'd often felt so desperate for him to fall asleep that I'm sure he felt my tension, and as a result was less likely to drop off. But viewing these pre-sleep times as worship seemed to help us both relax. Ben was so active the rest of the time that these minutes became all the more precious. And thinking about him and a coming baby was about as good an intro into the greatness of God as I could conjure.

Piercing the Shrink-Wrap

These moments of worship at home were very satisfying, but I wasn't ready to give up on church worship yet. There's something about music in particular that can carry away large groups as we all sway on an emotional tide, becoming greater together than the sum of our parts. The trouble was, I didn't seem to get myself to this place at our church, which I loved in every other respect. I knew it was possible, having experienced such a phenomenon many other times. Was such a feeling just emotional manipulation or was it really true worship? Maybe some emotional manipulation was involved, but I truly believed that God reached our hearts this way if we opened them to him. In *Our Greatest Gift*, Henri Nouwen describes two ways that we feel joy, and both are intimately connected with community. One is to acutely feel how different we are from those around us and the other is to acutely feel how we are all the same, what Nouwen terms "the immense joy of being a member of the human race." Nouwen considers the latter the more important, and it is certainly the feeling we get when we raise our voices together to praise our God, who is so much bigger than we even can imagine.

One of the first times I ever heard contemporary praise music was the summer before my junior year of high school, when I attended a work camp with my church youth group. Every night, the camp leaders put on a full-scale program, complete with set, multimedia, and a worship band augmented with a powerful sound system. As I sang the words that marched across the projection screen—"Awesome God," for one—my heart assented to God in a way I had never felt before. I had been a cradle Christian, and intellectually accepted my faith as a high school freshman when I was confirmed, but these worship services seemed to provide a missing piece of my faith—a feeling of God being with me, with all of us, that was intoxicating. My heart swelled along with the music. I felt very small and very large all at the same time.

These feelings were what I thought of as worship, and they hadn't been limited to my worship experiences as a teenager. Actually, I had just experienced this powerful physical sense of God's presence at the worship service the last morning of the Renovaré conference the month before. It was the first morning session I'd felt well enough to attend, and feeling better, and also being done with my talks, put me in a pretty joyful starting place. The service began with Renovaré president Chris Webb standing alone in the center of the large auditorium stage, dressed in his brown Franciscan robes, leading us all in a hauntingly beautiful a cappella song I'd never heard before. We did a kind of call-and-response, which then moved seamlessly into some lightly accompanied music that made me want to stomp and clap my hands, hoedown style. The service went on to hit everything from "Amazing Grace" to liturgical dance to the more typical leader-led worship with an accompanying band and praise songs. It was the worship version of the "all of the above" box. I felt my hands rising of their own accord, something I don't often do in my home church since it is not a typical part of Presbyterian worship. (There's a reason they call Presbyterians the frozen chosen.) But there's something about physically reaching for God that feels like a powerful and public way to ask God to enter your body, your soul, your life. I felt as though I'd asked God to do so that day.

Why didn't I feel this powerful emotional connection every Sunday in church? It was certainly nothing the worship leader or pastor was doing wrong. *I* could do better. I could and should continue to better prepare myself by focusing on God and seeking to open my heart.

But I also concluded that this emotional connection I sometimes felt through music was just one way of experiencing worship. And that as nice as the feeling was, it wasn't something that I should go to church expecting, or come away disappointed over when it didn't materialize. These powerful emotional experiences were a gift from God, made all the more meaningful because they were not all that frequent. But they were just one of the gifts of connecting with God in worship—others were reflecting on God's greatness through his word or through shared prayer or through time with Ben.

Music is not irrelevant, far from it. There's an important reason Moses and the Israelites sang a victory song to God after their escape from Egypt, with Miriam and the other women playing the tambourine and dancing; why David played the lyre, set aside a group of people as temple musicians, and wrote so many beautiful psalms with lines such as "Sing to the LORD a new song!" Music can open our souls to God's greatness in a mysterious and powerful way, but limiting my idea of experiencing worship solely to music and to emotion was a mistake, and one that could lead to my only wanting to experience God, or feeling that I had experienced God when there was an emotional payoff. After all, feelings weren't the point. God was. As Eugene Peterson writes, "If Christians worshiped only when they felt like it, there would be precious little worship. . . . Worship is an *act* that develops feelings for God, not a *feeling* for God that is expressed in an act of worship. When we obey the command to praise God in worship, our deep, essential need to be in relationship with God is nurtured."

Sometimes I feel as if all week long I become increasingly wrapped in a plastic shrink-wrap of materialism and to-do lists until I'm like one of those plastic sofas that you can spill freely on because they never absorb anything. And sometimes it seems to me that the purpose of coming to church is simply to pierce that wrapping. When a phrase or a verse or a song does get through to my heart, then it's always accompanied by such a sense of relief. Relief that I am really feeling and thinking about what matters. Then I start to picture what it might really be like for God's kingdom to come, and although at times that image fails to excite me, wrapped as I am in the comfort and complacency of the everyday, sometimes I catch a glimpse of how much more beautiful for all people the world could be, how much less pain, how much more love, and tears sting my eyes, washing away a layer of plastic.

My job is just to come back. Set a date with God, and then keep it.

Non-Expert Tips for Practicing Worship

1. When you attend church, look forward to meeting God there. Prepare yourself with a feeling of expectation.

2. And yet . . . don't hesitate to claim worship where you find it, especially when it is with your children.

3. Don't fall into the trap of thinking that you are worshiping only if you are having an emotional reaction.

4. And yet . . . cherish those times when you feel that connection to God with your whole body. Praise God for your emotions. Fickle and untrustworthy as they can be, they are still a gift.

8

FAILURE AND FASTING: GIVING SOMETHING UP TO RECEIVE GOD'S GIFTS

October

In his fasting, therefore, let a man rejoice inwardly in the very fact that by his fasting he is turning away from the pleasures of the world to make himself subject to Christ.

—Augustine of Hippo

My morning sickness eased a little after I got home from the conference, but it came back in full force in August. I spent most of August and September lying on the cool tiles of the bathroom floor or curled in a ball on the couch while Ben watched *Quick Pitch* on the Major League Baseball channel. Being a vessel for a new baby was more exhausting than I had remembered. I spent much of my nonsick time researching how to be less sick. I put crackers on the table beside the bed. I tried eating immediately before bed and first thing when I woke up. I took ginger, in candied and pill form. I'm not sure any of it really helped, but eventually the sickness waned and then passed almost entirely.

The upside of my sickness was that Ben's batting swing was looking more and more like Ryan Howard's, and we were both learning a lot about baseball. The downside was that I had not managed to practice solitude and fasting as I had planned, at least not in a way that had yielded any spiritual insights.

By October, I was in that second-trimester sweet spot where I started to feel better and more energetic. I even started to look pregnant instead of merely chubby. I was a successful baby incubator but a failing spiritual practitioner. Determined to get back on track, I decided to move ahead with another spiritual practice I had been dreading: fasting.

Fasting is one of those spiritual practices that is frequently mentioned in the Bible but rarely practiced today. Jesus spoke about it with the words "*When* you fast . . ." (Matthew 6:16, emphasis added), clearly assuming that everyone he was speaking to (every good Jew) had a solid fasting practice. Fasting was done communally during certain days in the Jewish religious calendar, but it was also practiced during times of special need. At times fasting seemed to be a sort of preparation, like Jesus' fast of forty days and forty nights before he began his ministry. In other times it seemed to be a first response in times of trouble, with varying results. Esther and her maids and all the Jews in Persia fasted in response to a plot to kill the Jews, and the plot was thwarted. David fasted when his child by Bathsheba fell ill. He ended his fast when the child died. Scripture makes it clear that fasting was always expected to be accompanied by prayer. As Timothy Simpson explains, "The theological significance in each case [of biblical fasting] seems to be that the denial of bodily needs for specified periods of time focuses the soul for greater attentiveness to God."

Fasting was *not* my instinct when times got hard or when I wanted to be especially attentive to God. Instead, I have to admit, I viewed fasting as a kind of relic from earlier Christian asceticism—something that the desert fathers did, right alongside depriving themselves of sleep and perching on poles for great swaths of time, like a very early version of *Survivor*. Although I had done brief group fasts several times and partial fasts during Lent, for me fasting from food was always tangled up with appearance and weight loss. I spent so much of my fasting time thinking about how I might lose a few pounds or, conversely, how I might slow and damage my metabolism, that I feared I was missing out on a lot of the spiritual benefits. I am not alone in these ideas. Whether it's because we are not used to denying ourselves much of anything or whether we fear for our health or whether we are rebelling against overly ascetic practices in earlier Christian generations, for most of us fasting isn't on our top five list of spiritual practices. At least not enjoyable ones.

When I talked to other moms about fasting, they tended to groan. Almost all said they didn't fast, at least not from food. For them, like me, fasting was too wrapped up in body image and appearance. And they didn't feel they had the luxury of taking a day without calories with demands on their body like breastfeeding, crazy schedules of chauffeuring the kids here and there, or simply the physical exertion of running after their kids. Not to mention the fact that in most households mothers were responsible for all the meals and the snacks. It's tough to fast from food when you need to provide three meals and umpteen snacks for others.

I could relate to all these concerns about fasting. But I kept returning to the fact that Jesus managed to fast—and for forty days. And the gospel writers made clear that for Jesus, being fully human, this fasting was as difficult as it would have been for any of us. Luke point-blank tells us that afterward, "Jesus was starving." I also couldn't get past the way Jesus spoke about fasting in the Sermon on the Mount, with such casually offered instructions that it seemed clear he expected the rest of us to do so too:

When you fast, don't put on a sad face like the hypocrites. They distort their faces so people will know they are fasting. I assure you that they have their reward. When you fast, brush your hair and wash your face. Then you won't look like you are fasting to people, but only to your Father who is present in that secret place. Your Father who sees in secret will reward you. (Matthew 6:16-18)

I liked the idea that fasting was something to be done privately just between me and God. I also couldn't help but notice that to Jesus, it seemed, fasting was to be done using another spiritual practice—secrecy—in order to ensure that it wasn't practiced just so that others could see what a spiritual giant you were.

An Alternative Fast

Fasting from food was clearly important, but my pregnancy made it impossible for me to try it. I would have to abstain from something else, such as media or technology. An alternative fast such as these, although obviously not directly referenced in Scripture, seemed in line with the biblical principles of fasting, namely, giving up something for the purpose of increased focus on God.

I knew immediately what I should fast from: TV, mostly because I felt a real resistance to the idea of entirely abstaining from it. I had learned that similar strong feelings of resistance were often clues that something was becoming unhealthy. I didn't watch much if any TV during the day, with the exception of letting Ben watch the MLB channel when I had been so sick, but nighttime was a different story. Ryan and I were so physically and emotionally exhausted after our days that immediately following Ben's bedtime we collapsed on the couch in front of the TV. We usually watched a program or two together until one or sometimes both of us fell asleep. Obviously I liked the shows I watched—some dramas, some comedies, some reality TV like *Top Chef* and *Project Runway*—or I wouldn't be watching them, but even I had to admit half-sleeping on the couch while I took in these shows was not the most spiritually fulfilling way to spend an evening.

How Much Is Too Much?

Still, I struggled with setting parameters for my fast, mostly because of my own reluctance to do this thing all the way. I told myself giving up TV entirely would be hard on Ryan because, after all, watching a DVR'd show or a movie was one of our nighttime rituals, unhealthy as it may have been. If I'm not around or am working, Ryan will just watch Fox Soccer. He could watch Fox Soccer all day, unless of course he finds an uplifting sports movie on cable. If *Remember the Titans* is playing on any channel whatsoever, we *will* watch it. For the forty-eighth time.

What Works for Me

Clarissa, high school math teacher and mom of three

After years of being pregnant or nursing, this was one of the first years that I've fasted during Lent by one day a week only eating two very small meals. One of the biggest things is that all day it makes you think about God. In general, we pray before we eat, but I don't think about God the entire time I'm eating. But those fasting days, I think about how this is for God. I feel like I'm honoring God, and it makes me feel joyful.

But here's the thing: before we met, Ryan didn't even have a TV. He joked that owning a TV would cause him to flunk out of law school. *I* was the one who introduced the TV to our house after we got married, and so deep down I knew he would be glad to give it up if I asked him. I was the one who didn't want to give it up, a point that was brought home to me when I was trying to work out the specifics of my fast from TV. Would I fast during the week and then watch on the weekends? Would I fast just from TV, so movies or Internet stuff would be OK? Would I just try to "do my best"? OK, even I knew that last one was nothing but a fasting cop-out.

One night while I was thinking this through, Ryan brought home some work. Since he didn't have an office in our house, he had to sit at our table to work, ten feet from the television. Instead of feeling sad that he had to spend his evening working, I instead felt annoyed that I couldn't watch one of the shows I had DVR'd while I folded the laundry. Folding the laundry is my favorite household task. It is a rare opportunity to take a basket of messiness and make it organized and neat. I find it very satisfying. Plus, I always save it for after Ben's bedtime so I can watch TV while I fold, which allows me to feel better about watching TV in the first place. Oh, the multitasking never ends.

That night, with three loads of laundry to fold, I felt oh-so-put-upon that I couldn't watch TV while I did it. Even as I noticed with a kind of detached concern that it should not be that big of a deal, somehow it felt like it was.

Clearly something needed to change.

I decided that I would give up TV during the week, on "school" nights, but that Ben could still watch his one show and that Ryan and I could watch on weekend nights. That way, we could still watch movies together. We had a DVR, so really it wasn't even that much of a sacrifice. I could watch the shows I liked on the weekend or after the month was over. That first night, Ryan was out of town on business, so I put Ben to bed and did a few things around the house, cleaning up the kitchen and so forth. Then I read on the couch. I felt like I was in *Charlie and the Chocolate Factory* when the Oompa Loompas sing the song about the television-addicted Mike Teavee, in which they ask rhetorically what all the children did before TV. Why, they read, of course!

After an hour or so, I was pretty much done, and I went to bed. At 9:30. I felt almost like a pioneer woman, going to sleep with the sun. I think it was safe to say that was the earliest I'd been to bed since Ben's infant days when I would claim any available minute for sleeping. I felt pretty good about my no-TV day until I realized that earlier, at the gym, I'd watched TV on the screen while I worked out on the elliptical trainer. I hadn't even noticed.

That evening schedule became typical. I put Ben to bed, cleaned things up, read for a while, and then went to bed ridiculously early. I felt better rested than I had, well, since he'd been born. It was funny. I'd always been incredibly protective of that time after Ben went to bed because I could finally do *my* stuff. (Oh yes, my practice of submission was still serving me well.) Sometimes I just could not *wait* for him to fall asleep so that I could do what I wanted.

Except, I now reflected in my TV-free time, what I wanted to do after his bedtime didn't always turn out to be all that fun. Sometimes it was working, which was of course necessary, but most of the time it was watching TV or a movie in a heap on the couch. Most of the time I fell asleep, at least partially, and then still tried to blink my way through the show just so I could be done with it and delete it. In a way, the shows on the DVR had become yet another item on my to-do list. I had to be sure to watch before they were automatically deleted because if not, I might never get to watch them. And what a tragedy *that* would be.

Fasting is meant to focus your attention. Very quickly I saw that not only was my typical TV watching not bringing me much spiritual fulfillment, I wasn't even enjoying it.

When Ryan got back from his business trip, he reiterated how excited he was about my no-TV plan. (Obviously, thinking giving up TV would be hard on him had been the flimsiest of excuses—ah, the lies we tell ourselves!) We sat on the couch with mugs of tea and actually talked about our days. OK, mostly I talked. Ryan was already accustomed to the verbal floods I often unleashed on him in the evenings after a day of talking to no one but Ben, and he listened patiently to all my cute little Ben stories, you know, the ones that are endlessly fascinating—but only to parents. Then we both went to bed early.

When the weekend arrived, I felt a little nervous about watching TV again, like just one show could now be the gateway drug that knocked me right back to where I had started. That fear was not altogether implausible. I soon got right back into the TV rhythm and watched several shows that had piled up on my DVR. On the bright side, I folded all the clean laundry that had also been piling up.

A visit from my parents offered more insight into my TV habit. One afternoon, while I was in the shower, my mom turned on a typical Lifetime movie. Couple tempted by adultery! Teenage daughter in trouble! When I got out of the shower, I sat on the couch and stared at it with her. After a few minutes, my mom said, "Why are we watching this? I wanted to talk to you!" "I don't know," I said. "It's pretty awful." But we were hooked into the awfulness, and we still sat there watching the movie until it was time to go to dinner. I was no better at turning off the TV then than I was all those nights I was falling asleep on the couch. Attempting to control my TV watching with my fasting practice helped me realize that much of the time TV seemed to control me.

After my parents left, for the first time I had to fight the urge to turn on the TV. I really wanted to watch a show while I picked up the living room, which was its usual post-visit disaster. I always tried to get the place neat for a parental visit, but then while my parents were actually here, I seemed to have so much less time for daily maintenance that the house was always in crisis mode by the time they left.

And it wasn't just accompaniment for housekeeping that I craved. Like the way I'd uncharacteristically turned on that documentary the afternoon after my sister's family visit earlier in the year, I realized that I liked to use TV as a way to unwind and turn my brain off for a while after a busy or stressful time. For introverted me, socializing, even with my parents, counted as a busy and stressful time. It wasn't that I hadn't thoroughly enjoyed myself during the busyness of their visit. I had. But now that the visit was over, watching TV was the way I wanted to give myself a break.

I was going to have to figure out some other ways to unwind.

After a while, however, I noticed that my fasting practice had helped me build up some resistance. When the next weekend came, I noticed that I didn't want to watch as many shows. Just one or two seemed like more than enough after not watching any all week. As a result, my DVR started to become clogged up. I stopped taping some of the reality shows I'd really liked, such as *Project Runway*. I didn't have the time to dedicate to it, and I found that as much as I enjoyed watching these talented designers transform coffee filters and doggy treats into clothing, I didn't feel like watching all the little quarrels and intrigues along the way. This seemed like a victory or, at least, progress.

The most surprising thing about my (okay, partial) fast from TV? How much I enjoyed it. I guess I shouldn't have been so surprised. I had made it easy on myself by restricting my fast to weeknights, but then again, one of the keys to practicing any spiritual discipline is setting a goal that is reasonable. Otherwise, you may never get anywhere. There were times in the middle of the week when I really wished I could just watch one tiny little show, but one result of restricting my TV consumption was that I truly enjoyed and appreciated those times when I did get to watch a movie or a show with Ryan on the weekends. And we both enjoyed the extra time we had in the evenings to talk. One night he'd had a long day at work and I could tell he really wanted to watch TV so I told him to go ahead and turn on Fox Soccer, which he happily did, and I sat next to him and read. Both of us were content.

Maybe there's another reason why Jesus instructed those who fast not to put on sad faces. Maybe it was because fasting is meant to be joyful, both by renewing your appreciation for what you are setting aside and through the increased attentiveness to God that is at its heart.

I had thought of fasting as sacrificing, that *I* was the one who was giving, but through my fast I received the gift of time—time I was able to use for increased quality time and conversation with my spouse, reading, and rest. Every night after a little bit of reading and talking to Ryan, what I really seemed to want to do was go to sleep. And with the extra rest I was getting, I felt a lot better. I was more patient, less likely to fall asleep while reading a pre-nap or pre-bedtime story, and just flat-out had a more cheerful outlook. I had known I needed more rest, but I'd hated the idea of giving up the "me" time in the evening. It turned out, though, that the "me" time was more accurately described as "TV" time because when I wasn't watching TV, I couldn't seem to care less about "me" time; I just wanted to go to bed.

Still, was sleeping how I should be spending my fasting time? Should I have been instead studying or praying more? Then again, I remembered the words of a contemplative prayer writer who comforted those who fell asleep during their attempted practice, saying that perhaps God wanted them to have a holy nap. I concluded that God may well have wanted me to get some extra rest.

I felt, however, that I should use at least some of my TV-free time for a more intentional way of connecting with God. So one night I settled at the dining room table with my tower of clean laundry, vowing to fold it all in silence, with no radio or iPod music, praying over each piece and its owner. And to like it, by gosh!

I soon realized I might have picked the wrong load with which to begin this practice. It seemed to be all gym clothes. At first I prayed earnestly over each workout top and each pair of my husband's soccer shorts, and then, well, I started to tire of thanking God for my healthy body and for Ryan's strong legs and love of soccer. I wondered if even God might be tired of my increasingly tepid prayers, and I started instead to ponder the impressive number of workout tops I had amassed and to wonder when Ryan had managed to wear so many pairs of soccer shorts anyway. Was he playing soccer in the middle of the night?

But then my thoughts drifted to a friend who was sick and other friends who were leaving our church, and I started to pray for them.

Then God seemed to bring other people to my mind, and I prayed for them too. It wasn't that I hadn't prayed for them before or that I wouldn't have prayed for them otherwise, but the quiet and the rote activity had created space in which I could pray for them in a way that felt meaningful and effective. Kathleen Norris describes how daily tasks can lead to prayer in her book *The Quotidian Mysteries: Laundry, Liturgy and "Women's Work."* She describes the motion and the repetition of tasks such as walking, baking bread, or doing laundry as offering both a rhythm for prayer and also the space and freedom for our minds to brainstorm. That had certainly been true for me. I finished the folding and gathered up the clothes to put away. It hadn't gone exactly the way I'd expected, but then what in my spiritual life ever did? It was a continual lesson for me. Open yourself up to God, and God will guide you along the path you need to travel—not necessarily the one you planned, but the one that will lead you Godward.

Non-Expert Tips for Practicing Fasting

1. Set reasonable fasting expectations for yourself, especially when you are beginning a practice. You will likely give yourself a better chance of following through and having a meaningful experience if you don't start out by trying to fast from food for a week or go completely media-free for a month. After all, you're trying to connect with God, not impress God. Right?

2. Be mindful of what takes the place of what you are giving up.

3. Listen to the insights God gives you about the hold whatever you are fasting from may have on your life, and ways you might be able to restore it to its proper place when your fast is ended.

4. Think of fasting less as a sacrifice on your part than as a new way to open yourself to receiving God's good gifts.

9

SERVICE: HELPING CLOSE TO HOME

November

Then Jesus took a towel and a basin and redefined greatness.
—Richard J. Foster, *Celebration of Discipline*

I felt like I was in a "taking" period of life. At church I needed child care anytime I wanted to attend anything. I took advantage of MOPS, Bible study, and Sunday school for Ben. The list went on and on. I took everything, and I gave nothing. At least that's how I was beginning to feel.

It wasn't that I didn't think I should be taking advantage of all those opportunities—far from it. The child care was a great outreach to the young families my church was always trying to welcome, and it was offered freely, never grudgingly. It was just that I wanted to be able to give too.

Ever since I could remember, I'd always felt that I was serving the Church in some concrete way. But as was the case with so many other spiritual practices, I wasn't sure how to do it anymore in my life as mom of Ben and his soon-to-be-born little brother. And that was troubling because, to me, service is at the very heart of what it means to follow Jesus. If you want to be like Jesus—you serve others.

How *did* you engage in service outside the home as a mom with a small child? It no longer seemed feasible to head off for a week of service in some faraway place, like I'd done almost every summer since I was a teenager. Even volunteering at the local homeless shelter felt like it was out of reach—I had been in enough homeless shelters to know that I wasn't quite ready to take Ben to one yet. When I stepped back and thought about it, it appeared that the only service I had done since Ben's birth was service to other moms. Mom service involved things that were more mundane, although possibly as important— making meals for other moms who were sick or who had just had new babies, or trying to support others who had trouble breastfeeding, as I had. My own lack of community and help when I'd had Ben underscored the importance of this kind of help.

But it seemed that I should be doing more. (Didn't it always?) And I wanted to be more deliberate about practicing service to show Ben what service to others meant and why we did it. Plus, with a new little brother on the way, I felt it was urgently important for Ben to realize that other people had needs too. Lately, we seemed to be engaged in a constant tug-of-war. I wanted him to get ready to go; he said, "No!" I tried to carry him; he started flailing and hit me. Anything I wanted him to do, he immediately and sometimes violently rejected. I had started giving myself mommy time-outs to calm myself down after these power struggles.

In fact, I was becoming quite the master of the mommy time-out.

And I couldn't stop thinking about how all this was going to play out with a newborn in the house. Likely, Ben, who couldn't help but notice the consistent progress of my stomach, was worried about the same thing. We both needed to shift the focus from our own needs to the needs of others.

November seemed like an auspicious time to do so—all kinds of service opportunities arise around the holidays as people start thinking about others who don't have a family or a Thanksgiving dinner or a Christmas tree or even a house in which to place their tree.

When a program at our church asked for donations of new toys for Christmas gifts for children of military families, it seemed like a great way to talk to Ben about helping others. So one day when we were on our way home from preschool, I told him that we were going to buy some toys and give them to some children who didn't have many toys.

His immediate response? "No! I want the toys!"

"Ben, you have plenty of toys. These will be extra toys for children who don't have any."

"No, they have toys! They have plenty of toys!"

I realized the concept of someone who didn't have a room full of toys like he and his friends did was completely foreign to him. I wasn't quite sure how to bring this point home, so I just kept talking to him about how we were going to give toys away to these kids who didn't have many toys. His resistance gradually started to recede. He went to the store with me and we picked out a baseball tee and pitching machine—a gift he himself would have liked to receive. Ben was excited about buying it and seemed to understand it wasn't for him, but once we had the box in our home, however, he really wanted to open it. I had to keep reminding him it was for another child.

Finally, Sunday came and we carried the toy to church. I dropped it in the donation box while he headed to Sunday school. Afterward, I took him over so he could see the toy there and reminded him that it was a gift from him for a little boy or girl who didn't have many toys, and for the first time he seemed excited about the idea. It didn't hurt that a girl who looked about ten was staffing the donation box and made a big fuss over how nice it was that he had given away such a nice toy. Lesson learned: sometimes the message needs to come from someone other than Mom.

And after all, my idea wasn't really to force Ben to practice service. I wanted to do it myself, to model it for him. And for me, too, frankly.

Saying Yes

Just as I was casting about for my own opportunity to serve, God sent an opportunity my way. I was asked to be a deacon at church. Not having grown up in the Presbyterian church, I wasn't even sure what that meant. In the church I'd grown up in, the deacons were the guys who mowed the lawn and shoveled the sidewalks—not necessarily a job I felt I was suited for with a small child and another one on the way. But the head of the deacons explained to me that it was more of a general service position—that it could involve anything from helping out with some of the children's ministry programs, to greeting at the church entrance and delivering flowers, to working with local soup kitchens or delivering cards or dinners to church members in need. Here was my chance to be not just a "taker" at church, a consumer of services like child care and the Young Marrieds group and MOPS, but someone who also gave. This opportunity sounded like a perfect way to practice service, and with Ben in tow.

Yet I hesitated.

I'd wanted to commit to a month of service, but deacons served three-year terms. With the new baby coming, I had thought I would be cutting back on commitments rather than adding to them. And even without a newborn in the picture, I was still feeling squeezed for time. Between my work obligations as writer and editor and my home obligations as a mom and a wife and the attendant housekeeping and cooking and cleaning and management responsibilities, I often felt a notepaper's width from going completely over the edge. Plus, Ben wasn't exactly the kind of kid who would patiently sit through a meeting with me. I even considered whether I was leading myself to some comeuppance of the chick lit sort. For example, I unwisely overextend myself and end up with Ben dialing 911 on my cell phone as I go into labor while trying to deliver flowers to an elderly shut-in.

On the other hand, I felt as though I'd gotten a free pass from all commitments of this type since Ben had been born, and I wasn't sure that was fair or appropriate. He was three now. And let's face it, I was still finding time to read and watch TV. I decided I needed to make time for something that really mattered. So many women's magazines seem to advise us not to overload ourselves—just say no to things you don't want to do! Well, this is probably good advice and a helpful corrective to many. But if I did only what I wanted to do, I wouldn't do much of anything at all—hardly a Christian way to go through life. Thomas R. Kelly wrote that we are not required to serve in every kind of ministry (to my great relief), but the corollary of this statement must be that when opportunities arise in the kind of ministry to which we think we are called, we should seriously consider those opportunities.

Being married with a small child, another on the way, and no family in town also requires the agreement of your husband before taking on any commitments of this nature. Just like with fasting, without even asking him, I pretty much concluded that it would be too hard on Ryan. His job was intense. How could he commit to being home while I attended weekly training meetings all this month and the next? Then, starting in January, three *years* of monthly meetings and accompanying activities?

Of course, when I finally stopped deciding that he couldn't do it and actually asked him, Ryan was all for it. Not only did he agree, he said enthusiastically that we would consider it our family's ministry and he would help me perform my duties whenever he could. Dallas Willard writes in *Hearing God* that God often speaks to us through people in our lives. In my life, that person is most often Ryan, which is good and lucky, since he's also the guy I talk to most. When would I learn to stop blaming him when I didn't want to do stuff? I was out of excuses. Besides, in addition to Ryan, I also heard God whispering to me that I should do this.

So I said yes.

You might have picked up on my pattern by now, one that seems to weave its way through every service opportunity that presents itself to me. An opportunity comes up. I think I should probably do it, but I waffle about it, worrying that it's too much or that I'm too busy, getting all worked up over it. Ryan responds with a version of "Of course you should do it. What are you waiting for?" And then, robbed of excuses, I sign up for said opportunity and find that it is wonderful. I am a slow learner.

Meetings Galore

I began my deacon training with a series of weekly meetings, during which we were trained in church policy, procedure, and theology, and also just what it is that deacons are supposed to do. These meetings were a lot more fun than my description makes them sound. Since Ryan knew I had to get to the meetings, he made an extra effort to come home early, and then I set off feeling footloose and fancy-free with a purse instead of a diaper bag to talk about theology and stuff for an hour or two while he put Ben to bed. The more I thought about it, the more I realized what a good deal it was for me.

As we discussed all the service opportunities, I was surprised and maybe even a little disappointed to see how many of them were directed at members of our own church. Yes, there were food drives and backpack drives and shoe drives for the larger community, but mainly our job was to serve those within our church with cards, meals, flower deliveries, pancake breakfasts, and so on. As we studied the history of the role of deacons, however, I was reminded that the first deacons were those seven men chosen from the members of the early church to make sure that the food was distributed properly, literally to wait on tables so the apostles didn't have to be bothered with such matters (Acts 6). Their job was to serve the people in their own community, just as we were asked to do in our church.

What Works for Me

Michelle, yoga teacher and mom of two

Before we open anything on Christmas, we gather these little presents that we've made, usually a tray of homemade cookies, and then a bag with a bottle of water and a poncho or sunscreen, and we go to a local street to pass them out to the homeless. This year we gave a bag to a homeless lady, and my daughter gave her a big hug. She is the hugging bandit. It's an amazing ministry she has. All of a sudden the lady comes back and gives my daughter a really old copy of *Black Beauty* and a bracelet. For everyone, it's important to be able to give.

The ways in which we were asked to serve were a lot like the things I had minimized as "mom" service. I realized I'd always felt service was something that I had to do for people who were Other—serving those who were extremely poor, good; serving those who were from a place very far away, even better. I had felt that if I wasn't serving people I didn't know, people who were clearly down and out, who were extremely poor or even homeless, that somehow it didn't count. What a foolish and limited idea of service. We serve where we are, however we can. Jesus healed the sick and directed his followers to help the poor, but it was the feet of his beloved disciples that he washed.

Just Do It

I was now fully on board with this kind of service, but I hadn't actually had to do any yet. Finally, my fellow deacons and I completed our training and were officially sworn in before the entire congregation. I wobbled on up to the front of the church in my maternity wrap dress and high-heeled boots that I could barely zip around my calves, and all the former elders and pastors in the church were called to the front to lay hands on us. My mother-in-law, an ordained Presbyterian minister, was visiting and came forward to lay her hands on my back as we promised to serve the church and were prayed over. I was mostly praying not to pass out as I reminded myself to unlock my knees, but it felt good to commit to doing something for others.

As I began my term, I realized that commitment seemed to make the difference. When ad hoc opportunities came up, I sometimes said yes, but more often I waffled, wondering whether we had plans I wasn't remembering or if a conflict might come up later, until someone else agreed to do it. It became pretty clear that I would waffle myself out of anything if given half the chance. So I just had to commit in advance and hope for the best.

My favorite type of service turned out to be one I had always considered mundane, "love baskets." For a long time I thought these were supposed to be gift baskets, but it turns out it just meant dinner. I remembered how hard it was to try to figure out dinner when Ben had been an infant, and so I always *wanted* to help with this kind of thing. But at the same time, I was neither a gifted cook nor the most organized person.

This is pretty much how it went every single time: I would attempt to plan ahead the menu and the shopping and the cooking time and everything else but would be stymied by work commitments or naps. I would do my best to cook, inevitably discovering that I was missing at least one vital ingredient, and everything would take way longer than I had planned. The process would be complicated by the fact that dinner-making hour was also the child witching hour when Ben (and every other kid I knew) was cranky, hungry, and tired all at the same time. I would try to entertain him and bribe him with snacks until the food was ready and packed. I would rush and sweat and check the time (how had this taken so long?) and complain in my head that I was never doing this again. Then I would double-check the directions only to find that the person I was delivering to lived much farther away than I thought they did. I would sweat some more and decide for certain that I was *never* doing this again. I would finally get in the car, only to be caught in traffic with a hungry, tired, and cranky child who wanted his own dinner, feeling terrible that the person whose meal we had made now had to wait to eat it. I would get lost twice before finally arriving and then be unable to find parking. I would find a spot many clicks away and hoof it, still sweating, with a disgruntled child and a rapidly cooling meal in tow.

Then, every time, the magic would happen.

The person answered the door, and cranky Ben would be transformed into a perfect, shy child. The recipient would be so delighted to receive the food and the visit that he or she would kindly overlook our tardiness, my sweatiness, and the questionable quality of the food. We would sit and have a brief chat in which Ben delighted because he was heavily featured and complimented, and during which I would hear about the situation of the person we were visiting and get all my own problems slammed into perspective. It would again become clear that the meal I stressed out so much over was entirely secondary to this: the visit. The sweat would cool, and I would cuddle Ben on my lap as he answered questions about how old he was and whether he had a brother or a sister in that large belly of his mother's, and eventually he would warm up enough to tell them about baseball and his favorite player, Ryan Howard.

Then we would head home, both quiet and calm and even forgetting to be hungry, so thankful to have been given the gift of being able to help someone else. I would think, *Why don't I do this more often?*

Non-Expert Tips for Practicing Service

1. Pay attention, because service opportunities come up constantly. And when they do come up, don't hesitate so long. After all, when's the last time you truly regretted helping someone or even just offering to do so?

2. Look for a regular commitment you can meet so you don't have to motivate anew each and every time.

3. Be open to less exotic, more everyday kinds of service. "Mom" service is service too.

4. Remember that service is at least as much for you as the other person. This helps keep you humble.

10

CELEBRATION: EXPERIENCING THE JOY OF THE EVERYDAY

December

*Celebration heartily done makes our deprivations and sorrows
seem small, and we find in it great strength to do the will of our
God because his goodness becomes so real to us.*
—Dallas Willard, *The Spirit of the Disciplines*

It may seem odd to think of joy as a spiritual practice. But of
course it is. Joy is a Christian virtue too. Jesus told his disciples: "I
have said these things to you so that my joy will be in you and your
joy will be complete."

So how do you practice joy, exactly? You celebrate. I think of
celebration as enjoying and appreciating all God has given us. Joy is
certainly connected to worship, but it's also meant to be a part of our
everyday lives. I've always liked Dallas Willard's words on the subject:
"We engage in celebration when we enjoy ourselves, our life, and our
world, *in conjunction with* our faith and confidence in God's greatness, beauty, and goodness. We concentrate on *our* life and world as
God's work and as God's gift to us." We are to enjoy ourselves, but his
words remind us of a certain deliberateness to the process. We place
our enjoyment in the context of our faith. We *concentrate*. So while
celebration can come to us spontaneously, we can also make a con-
scious decision to celebrate. That's what I planned to do in December.

What better month to practice celebration than December when, with the season of Advent and the approach of Christmas, people seem to feel festive and joyful? I was feeling festive and joyful myself, having just met another book deadline at the beginning of the month. Foremost in my mind was celebrating Christmas in our own house for the very first time. Ryan and I had always traveled to either his or my parents' home for Christmas, but with the baby due at the end of February, I was no longer in flying shape. This year it would be just the three of us for Christmas morning, with my parents flying in at noon on Christmas and Ryan's family coming for New Year's Eve. We had hired a contractor to build a wooden entertainment center and book-shelf unit in our main living area, so our home would look, we hoped, especially nice. I looked forward to hanging our stockings from the new shelves and making a special Christmas for Ben. It would be his last Christmas as an only child. Come February, things were going to change, for him and for all of us.

My first opportunity to practice celebration was a women's holi-day tea advertised in our church bulletin. I invited my friend Sara to go with me, but unfortunately she had to cancel on the day of the tea. Frankly, going alone didn't seem too celebratory. I knew I was now likely to be the only one under sixty. What would I even talk about with the other attendees? But I dragged my shy, reluctant self to our church's fellowship hall. As I walked in, I saw that I had guessed right about the room's general demographic. It was a collection of older women gathered around tables decorated with brightly colored paper place mats, pinecones, and trays of fruit bread and cookies. Christ-mas songs were playing, and the place felt warm and welcoming, and about as Christmassy as San Diego can get. A smiling woman I didn't know approached me almost immediately, grabbed my hand, and asked me to get a name tag. I guess it was fairly obvious that I was the new face in the crowd. She then directed me to a table with a couple of other very nice women. We chatted about e-mail and keeping in touch with family as we nibbled on butter cookies.

Then a woman sat down at the piano and started playing. I thought she was going to give a concert, but instead she started leading us in Christmas carols. When we got to "The Twelve Days of Christmas," she assigned each of us a line. My table partner and I got "two turtle doves." That meant we had to sing our little duet eleven times! As I've mentioned, I do not have the greatest singing voice, and in any other atmosphere I would have felt very self-conscious, but whether it was because we were all laughing or because I knew a few of the ladies couldn't hear very well, I soon realized I was having a great time. There was something irresistible about being so warmly welcomed by these ladies who were making such a heroic effort to include me.

Celebration in the Bible is about community. It's about weddings, feasting, dancing, singing. It's about connection. It doesn't take place alone. Anyone who's ever accomplished something big and immediately wanted to share it with someone else knows that. It was an unexpected and joyful gift for me to feel that I was part of a community that day. It was a good beginning to my practice of celebration.

Managing Expectations

It's the same every Christmas. As much as I love all the elements of the season, I quickly end up feeling buried under the list of things I haven't yet done. At the beginning of the month, I'd been pleasantly anticipating a nice family Christmas, happy that I had turned in a draft of my latest book, *A Year with Aslan*, but before I knew it, the month was hurtling on toward Christmas, and I hadn't completed any of those celebratory Christmastime tasks—decorating the house, buying a tree, organizing presents. It always seems as though the time between Thanksgiving and Christmas passes at warp speed, but I also know that when I don't have a deadline, I don't get all that much done. Give me a boatload of unrealistic expectations and I will deliver, but give me some nice time off with just a few things to do, and I won't manage any of them. It's a tiny bit maddening.

I'd never been a big home decorator, especially for holidays, and it hadn't mattered all that much because we'd always spent Christmas elsewhere. This year, however, I'd planned to all of a sudden pay attention to all of those decorating things you were supposed to do. I'd even anticipated the decorating process as a celebration in and of itself. But our pre-holiday renovation project, the built-in wooden entertainment center and bookshelves, threw a big wrench in my decorating plans. As is so often the case with contractors, ours had been delayed on other projects. The room where our unit was supposed to go was also the future site of the tree and stockings, so we put it all on hold until he was free. My to-do list was showing a serious lack of checks.

And despite the early high of the Christmas tea party, I was struggling to put myself in a celebratory frame of mind. Early in the month, I had a bit of a scare with my pregnancy. I had made what I thought was a routine call to my endocrinologist to confirm that she'd received my faxed thyroid levels from the OB. (I have a thyroid condition called Graves' disease, which causes my thyroid to run amok but is generally easily controlled by medication.) My endocrinologist said she hadn't received the results at all, or the ones from the previous test. As she checked my chart, her normally calm and lilting voice turned sharp.

She told me to come in first thing Monday, the next business day. All weekend I panicked about what was going on and whether the baby was okay, and on Monday all it turned out to be was that the latest research had indicated that patients like me should be on a different medication during the second and third trimesters. That was much better news than I'd anticipated, but the whole experience left me with a pervasive sense of unease. What else had I missed? Was everything really okay with that baby in there? Were *we* going to be okay with a newborn addition to our little family?

Why, when I was trying so hard to be celebratory, was I instead feeling drawn down into these worries? Ryan always joked that I was contrary, but this seemed a little extreme. Some of it had to be the constant reminder of my enormous belly. I also knew that thoughts like these often threatened to overwhelm me when Ryan was working hard, and lately he was working around the clock to try to finish various cases before the holidays. It felt hard to celebrate when I was, to tell the truth, lonely.

The Gigantic Joy

Preschool was over for the holidays, and it was time for Ben's first preschool Christmas recital. I was beyond excited and even a little nervous. Ben had just turned three—it was the first thing he'd ever had approaching a performance. Ryan met me there from work and we sat perched at the edges of our seats with the other preschool parents, practically trembling with anticipation. Then the back doors of the church were thrown open and all the three- and four-year-olds lined up at the back and marched in, singing "Jingle Bells" and shaking little bells. If any parent can watch that without crying little tears of pride and joy, then he or she must have a dry eye condition.

Ben, of course, had stripped off the preppy argyle V-neck sweater I'd put him in that morning and was down to his soccer T-shirt. As he marched by and spotted us in the pew, he grinned hugely and waved his jingle bells at us. It was clear he did not share my case of nerves. As the preschoolers performed their songs, I realized that he didn't quite seem to know the words, which bothered him not at all. He just followed the hand motions and beamed at us. I know our answering smiles were threatening to crack our faces in half. There is simply no greater joy than watching your child thoroughly enjoy himself.

After the show, all seven or so minutes of it, we joined Ben back in his classroom for a cookie party where Ben ate his first Rice Krispie treats, which he dubbed "sticky cookies." He could not get enough of them. There he sat at a miniature table in his messy T-shirt, stuffing cookies in his mouth and grinning, surrounded by his school friends and his teachers and beaming parents. It was one of those moments you want to freeze in time, when your child is truly, perfectly happy, happy as only children can be, and a part of you wants him to live forever in that moment, protected from the hurts and the heartaches that will come his way too early in life and too often. It reminded me of something I'd been told when I was pregnant, that having a child means your heart will forever be walking around outside your body. That sentiment also strikes me as theologically poignant. Isn't that what God did with Jesus—sent his heart out to be beaten up by the world? Isn't that how God feels about us?

It's funny how these moments of celebration are often tinged with an underlying feeling of sorrow. G. K. Chesterton writes, "Everything human must have in it both joy and sorrow; the only matter of interest is the manner in which the two things are balanced or divided." For the pagan, he goes on, joys are small and earthbound; while all things related to heaven must therefore be sad. In contrast, for the Christian, "joy becomes something gigantic and sadness something special and small."

Celebration seemed to come for me when I was linked by child or family or community to that pipeline of gigantic joy that is God. I felt a similar sense later that week when we walked up the street as a family, dachshund and all, to a block that has the best Christmas lights in San Diego. Ryan often commented that this spectacular Christmas effort must be stipulated in the mortgage agreements of every homeowner on that block. Every year they go all out—picture National Lampoon's *Christmas Vacation* multiplied by an entire neighborhood. You'd think all that excess would feel sad and over-commercialized, but the opposite was true. We walked up there in the mild winter weather, which even after years in San Diego still felt like spring to me, and boom, there was Christmas. Complete with fake snow and families strolling around in short sleeves and Santa on a surfboard. Whether it was the company or the lights or just being outside on a beautiful night, it felt more celebratory than any Christmas party we attended.

What Works for Me

Karen, mom of three

To me the best celebrations are thought up by the kids. My oldest daughter will say, "Mommy, can we have a tea party?" And I say, "Why not?" And so we set it up and they get so excited. It doesn't have to be elaborate or pre-planned. And those are the things they remember, not necessarily the things I spent a long time planning or the things that are large-scale.

The Carpenter's Gift

The week before Christmas, our carpenter finally told us that he had completed our shelves and entertainment center in his workshop and was ready to start installing them. It was great news. Except that in our small space, it meant Ben and I would have to work hard to stay out of his way. I had worried that it would be difficult to keep Ben from the siren song of power tools and large pieces of wood, but instead we had the best time camping out in my bedroom, reading through piles of books and napping together. In my third trimester now and starting to get tired again, I was only too happy to nap with Ben when possible.

The Sunday before Christmas we finally got our tree, which we had decided to stow in my office until the main room was ready. Ryan had to go to work straight afterward, so I waited for him to come home before decorating it, despite Ben's pleas to do it right then. I had in my head this kind of Martha Stewart moment where all three of us would drink hot chocolate, listen to Christmas music, and string lights and ornaments, but Ryan had to stay later than expected at work, almost until Ben's bedtime, and he also brought a friend home with him.

There went my cozy family decorating celebration.

Why had my husband ruined it? Well . . . because I hadn't actually *told* him my big decorating plans. I just assumed he would *know* that because we had purchased the tree that day, we would have a sitcom-style Christmas decorating party.

How many years did we have to be married before I realized that my husband could not, in fact, read my mind? Yes, just as Dallas Willard had advised, some deliberateness would have been helpful here.

If I wanted to have a celebration with my husband, I should at least have invited him to it.

As Ben and I instead decorated the tree together the next day, I watched how Ben's ability to live in the present contributed to a very real sense of joy and celebration. He wasn't waiting for Christmas morning in order to *really* have fun, and he certainly wasn't dwelling on any potential fun he had missed out on the night before. As much as I had erred by not fully articulating my ideas about the decorating celebration I had envisioned the night before, I also saw how I had meticulously loaded some future time with a pre-planned amount of celebrating expectations. And how such a practice was setting myself up not for joy, but for disappointment. While it was important to be deliberate about celebration, there was also a necessary element of spontaneity. I could have turned the previous night into a celebration, just a different one than I had originally envisioned. Instead, I had been too busy nursing my frustrated expectations, and there was nothing celebratory in that. Frustration and resentment are efficient destroyers of joy.

When things don't work out the way you want, it doesn't have to destroy joy. The practice of celebration is more about your reaction to these circumstances. You can deliberately choose joy and celebration, or you can deliberately choose to be annoyed. The sudden completion of our shelving unit seemed to prove this point.

Just when we had resigned ourselves to the construction continuing through the holiday, the project was finally completed, literally the afternoon of Christmas Eve. I had been so frustrated by the delayed project's interfering with the timeline of my celebration, but the truth was that the sudden completion of the project was an excellent Christmas gift, and from a carpenter, no less. All of a sudden our house was our own again, and it looked amazing with the freshly painted shelves and media center in the middle of it. Somehow the fact that the project had dragged on so long made Christmas feel like a sudden, and joyful, surprise. All three of us were running around, laughing, realizing how much we had to do still. Move the tree! Hang the stockings from the new shelving! Now it was time for the Christmas Eve service at church! And presents to be wrapped! And my parents flying in the next day for lunch!

When Christmas morning came, we all slept in, for probably the last time for many years. When Ben woke up and came to get us, he was excited to see presents under the tree and we all opened up a few gifts. Ben loved his new trains, play food, and books, and we loved watching him exclaim over them. But we were all waiting for something.

Finally, it was time to drive to the airport on deserted Christmas-morning streets to pick up my parents. As we spotted them standing on the sidewalk, Ben squealed and yelled and the dog whined and moaned. It was a loud and joyful car indeed that my mom and dad climbed into.

After all our excitement about having Christmas in our own home, with just us, somehow it didn't seem like a celebration until the rest of the family got there.

Following the short drive to our house and the requisite admiring of the new cabinetry, we all gathered at the table I had carefully set with a table runner and candles and our nicer wedding plates to eat steak and lobster tails from Costco. Ben was wearing shorts, the warm winter sunlight was slanting across our hastily decorated tree, and the dog was napping peacefully on the brand-new red Christmas tree skirt. It was that Christmas lunch, as we all crowded around our small table and made toasts to our soon-to-be-expanding family, that finally seemed like the celebration. And it was continued a few days later when we had a similar meal with Ryan's family. I kept thinking about the Nativity story, which includes a lot more people than just Jesus, Mary, and Joseph. Even in our little decorative Nativity scenes, the wise men and the shepherds and all the animals are always in there too. It is a downright crowded stable, but undoubtedly a place of joy. For a self-described introvert like me, it was quite the realization that every extra person or creature had the potential to multiply the joy. And it was a most poignant insight as I thought about it in terms of the upcoming arrival of our new son.

In the end, the most celebratory moments of the month were not the ones I had decided on ahead of time, and they weren't the ones centered around the stuff, like decorating the tree and opening Christmas presents or even Christmas parties. The celebrations were having tea and singing carols with some of the elder stateswomen at my church. Sitting with Ryan as we watched Ben sing in his recital. Reading books on my bed with Ben while the rest of our house was filled with wood shavings. Walking up the street as a family to look at the lights. Sharing a Christmas meal with my family and a New Year's Day meal with Ryan's family. They were all moments of connection with others, moments in which we could celebrate Jesus' birth and the anticipation of the birth of our new son.

Yes, you can plan celebrations. Of course you can. But you have to hold the little things, well, lightly. You're not celebrating the matched napkins or the completed furniture. You're celebrating the people. You're celebrating the gift from God of it all.

Richard Foster writes, "God's normal means of bringing his joy is by redeeming and sanctifying the ordinary junctures of human life."

Having a child both overwhelms you with the back-breaking weight of the mundane—the never-ending diapers, feedings, and laundry—and buoys you up with the powerful joy available in the ordinary—a smile in the rearview mirror, a giggle, a tiny toe. We may never be able to view every moment of life for the celebration that is its potential, but with practice we can shift the balance to fewer moments of feeling oppressed by the daily routine and more and more moments of sharing God's joy and celebration.

Non-Expert Tips for Practicing Celebration

1. Remember that celebration comes from sharing your joy with others, so plan time together.

2. Be open to spontaneous celebration.

3. Try not to place such high expectations on celebration occurring not now but at some fixed point in the future, exactly according to your plan. Joy is hard to schedule.

4. Remember that the potential for joy lies in the most ordinary moments of life.

CONCLUSION: GRACE AND MORE GRACE

On February 25, our new son was born. Late, like his brother. Although he entered the world at a reasonable-sounding 9:18 a.m., that time stamp of course leaves out the entire previous night of breathing, pain-reducing positioning, and not one but two trips to the hospital. Remarkably, again just like his brother, he was also the most perfect and gorgeous baby the world had ever seen. And again, his sweaty mess of a mother, characterized in photographs by her crazy raccoon eyes of smeared black mascara (note to self: you are not a Kardashian—you cannot get away with makeup during childbirth), was the proudest mom.

As every mother of two or more has discovered before me, you give yourself a bit of a break with the second child. When you first become a mother, there is just a dizzying amount of decisions to make. Your entire schedule has to be rebuilt from the floor up; you must choose what to prioritize and what to let slide. And all of it, every single bit of it, feels like it's of vital importance.

After you've been at it for a little while longer, you've already made a lot of those decisions. You've set the schedule and prioritized the priorities. You've also seen that, for the most part, things seemed to go fine even when you didn't make the baby food entirely from scratch or reach your 30,000-word target every single day. I no longer hold myself so entirely responsible for my child's every thought and developmental milestone. And by the same token, I have also tried to give myself a little bit of grace about the ups and downs of my year of spiritual practices. Every time I created a large expectation for myself, I didn't seem to be able to meet it, and then I felt even more guilty than I had before I started the whole endeavor. Those times when I set expectations that were more general or more manageable, I felt that God was able to work more freely in me. It's remarkable how much God teaches me when I just show up and pay attention.

Looking back, I can see some clear patterns. For those disciplines in which I had to add something to my schedule—study, contemplative prayer, or service, for example—I struggled. I had a much easier time with those that involved giving something up or just paying attention to the way something already worked in my life—silence, fasting, simplicity. Yet I chose fewer of those to practice. I seemed to have been laboring under the illusion that if I didn't have to struggle to carve out a dedicated slice of time for it, then it wasn't quite as worthwhile. It's also interesting that a spiritual discipline that is currently experiencing quite a resurgence, practicing the sabbath, didn't even cross my mind as one to practice. Perhaps rest was not in line with my own preconceptions of what a "discipline" should be.

When I talk to people about my year of practicing the disciplines, they often ask, "Well, did you keep on practicing each one even after the month was over?" I get the feeling they see the whole enterprise as a kind of house of cards, with the final discipline being laid precariously on top of all the rest and threatening to knock the whole house down. It wasn't like that in practice at all. The disciplines, of course, are not so differentiated and neatly categorized as we like to make them in books such as these. My practice of prayer informed my practice of silence, which offered insight into my practice of fellowship, and so forth and so on. They work together to help create a spiritual balance. And it's not so much a matter of adding one on top of the other but rather allowing each one to continue refining the central goals: connecting with God, becoming more like Jesus. Here I think of what Thomas R. Kelly writes in *A Testament of Devotion*: "Religion isn't something to be added to our other duties, and thus make our lives yet more complex. The life with God is the center of life, and all else is remodelled and integrated by it."

It was hard for me during this year, and it's still hard, to place God at the center of my life. I struggle with submitting to God's will; I want so much to be in charge, even as I recognize that I'm not doing that great of a job at it.

Every mother I know is hard on herself, and I am no exception. I am always thinking of what I can and should do, rather than what God has helped me do already or all the ways in which God has blessed me and my family. When I notice this tendency in my son, I remind him that he'll be a lot happier if he focuses on what he liked best about his day, rather than the one thing he didn't get to do. But it's no secret where he learned his focus on the things that didn't work out or what he didn't get right.

I wish I'd always focused more on what was right and good and praiseworthy about parenthood and my own attempts at it. I also wish I'd understood better from the beginning that parenting isn't something you can ace. It's a process. And so are the spiritual disciplines. We don't finish them or check them off our list. We return to them again and again. We throw ourselves back in the ring, and pray that we have opened ourselves to God enough to hear God's leading.

I've also realized that motherhood itself is about the most powerful spiritual discipline I've encountered. Ironically, the guy who showed me this lesson most clearly was Martin Luther. The Father of the Reformation seemed an unlikely source to teach about the spiritual essentialness of parenting, but in a sermon he gave in 1522 titled "The Estate of Marriage," he said,

> [When] our natural reason . . . takes a look at married life, she turns up her nose and says, "Alas, must I rock the baby, wash its diapers, make its bed, smell its stench, stay up nights with it, take care of it when it cries, heal its rashes and sores, and on top of that care for my wife, provide for her, labor at my trade, take care of this and take care of that, do this and do that, endure this and endure that, and whatever else of bitterness and drudgery married life involves?" . . .What then does Christian faith say to this? It opens its eyes, looks upon these insignificant, distasteful, and despised duties in the Spirit, and is aware that they are adorned with divine approval as with the costliest gold and jewels. It says, "O God, because I am certain that thou has created me as a man and hast from my body begotten this child, I also know for a certainty that it meets with thy perfect pleasure. I confess to thee that I am not worthy to rock the little babe or wash its diapers, or to be entrusted with the care of the child and its mother. How is it that I, without any merit, have come to this distinction of being certain that I am serving thy creature and thy most precious will? O how gladly will I do so . . . for I am certain that it is thus pleasing in thy sight."

Of course, this quote is aimed specifically at fathers, and I love the fact that Luther takes it for granted that in the sixteenth century dads are washing diapers and staying up all night with their babies! But what I really love about this quote is that it reminds me of the most important aspect of my life as a mom. Motherhood is a privilege and in itself a way of enriching my relationship with God. If I sit around all day worrying about not having enough time to study the Bible or to pray in a quiet place, I completely miss the point. My spiritual life is right here in the dirty diapers and the school lunches and the sleepless nights. God is using all this stuff to form me, and motherhood in itself is about as effective a spiritual tool as I know.

So I keep on getting shaped. And keep on.

ACKNOWLEDGMENTS

First and foremost, thanks to my wonderful family, my most amazing husband, Ryan, and my spiritual teachers Ben and Luke, who were so kind as to let me share their lives in a book. Great thanks also to my parents, Neal and Marilyn Roller, who have always supported me without reservation in any endeavor I put my mind to; and my loving and encouraging in-laws, Doug and Donna Waterman. Thanks to the talented ladies of the Coronado Writers Group, Krystee Kott and Carrie Keyes, for all the editing, encouraging, and commiserating. My appreciation and admiration to all the amazing women who have survived all these mothering experiences with me, especially my sister, Karen, who makes it all look so easy.

A gigantic thank you to my agent, Wendy Lawton of Books & Such, for believing in me and in this project. Thanks to the wonderful people at Abingdon—Lil Copan and Julie Gwinn—and my superb editor, Lauren Winner. And to everyone at Renovaré for their support, in particular Lyle SmithGraybeal, Richard J. Foster, Lynda Graybeal, Rachel Quan, and Joan Skulley.

In the interest of coherence, I have condensed some of the anecdotes related here into their respective months. Any mistakes are mine alone.

NOTES

Introduction: The Spiritual Crisis of Motherhood

p. xix Galatians 5:22-23 (NRSV). The fruit are "love, joy, peace, patience, kindness, generosity, faithfulness, gentleness, and self-control."

1. Prayer

p. 3 Epigraph: Dallas Willard, *The Spirit of the Disciplines: Understanding How God Changes Lives* (San Francisco: HarperOne, 1988), 185.

p. 3 See Psalms 5:3; 59:16; 88:13.

p. 4 Anonymous, *The Cloud of Unknowing,* trans. Carmen Acevedo Butcher (Boston: Shambhala, 2009), 11.

p. 5 A word here about contemplative prayer and my own theological background. A lot of people feel like contemplative prayer is not Christian—that it is instead some kind of New Agey meditation. This assumption is not true. Contemplative prayer has a rich history within the Christian tradition, from *The Cloud of Unknowing* to Teresa of Avila and her *Interior Castle*, to name just two. Yet I, too, had my moments of feeling a little weirded out by the idea of prayer that was more about listening than talking. So my solution is to use *Jesus* as my "centering word." Focusing on Jesus makes me feel safe.

p. 7 Evelyn Underhill, *Essential Writings* (Maryknoll, NY: Orbis, 2003), 125–26.

p. 8 Dallas Willard, *Hearing God: Developing a Conversational Relationship with God* (Downers Grove, IL: InterVarsity Press, 1999), 17.

p. 11 See http://ignatianspirituality.com/ignatian-prayer/the-examen/.

p. 13 Matthew 7:7-11, for example.

p. 13 Matthew 26:39: Mark 14:36.

p. 14 Quoted in Richard J. Foster and Emilie Griffin, eds., *Spiritual Classics: Selected Readings on the Twelve Spiritual Disciplines* (San Francisco: HarperOne, 2000), 39.

p. 17 Herbert F. Brokering, ed., *Luther's Prayers* (Minneapolis: Augsburg, 1994), 17–18.

p. 20 Underhill, *Essential Writings*, 126.

2. Fellowship

p. 26 Dietrich Bonhoeffer, *Life Together: The Classic Exploration of Christian Community* (San Francisco: HarperOne, 1954), 23.

p. 37 Henri J. M. Nouwen, *Letters to Marc about Jesus* (San Francisco: HarperOne, 1988), 43.

3. Submission

p. 43 Epigraph: Anne Lamott, *Help, Thanks, Wow: The Three Essential Prayers* (New York: Riverhead, 2012), 37.

p. 43 Mark 8:34.

p. 44 Richard J. Foster, Dallas Willard, Walter Brueggemann, and Eugene H. Peterson, eds., *The Life with God Bible* (San Francisco: HarperOne, 2005), 533.

p. 49 Quoted in John McPhee, "Editor & Publisher," *New Yorker*, July 2, 2012, 37.

4. Study

p. 61 Epigraph: Richard J. Foster, Dallas Willard, Walter Brueggemann, and Eugene H. Peterson, eds., *The Life with God Bible* (San Francisco: HarperOne, 2005), xxviii.

p. 61 Richard J. Foster, *Celebration of Discipline*, rev. ed. (San Francisco: HarperOne, 1998), 71.

p. 62 Deuteronomy 17:18-20.

p. 63 Daniel Hames, "Three Reasons Why You Don't Read Your Bible," found online at http://www.theologynetwork.org/bible-reading/three-reasons-why-you-dont-read-your-bible.htm.

p. 68 Matthew 3:7 NRSV.

p. 69 Matthew 5:42 NRSV.

p. 71 Rob Bell, *Velvet Elvis: Repainting the Christian Faith* (New York: HarperCollins, 2005), 40.

5. Simplicity

p. 79 Epigraph: Richard J. Foster, *Celebration of Discipline*, rev. ed. (San Francisco: HarperOne, 1998), 79.

p. 80 Richard J. Foster, Dallas Willard, Walter Brueggemann, and Eugene H. Peterson, eds., *The Life with God Bible* (San Francisco: Harper-One, 2005), 531.

p. 80 Foster, *Celebration of Discipline*, 88-89.

6. Silence

p. 95 Epigraph: Blaise Pascal, *Pensées*, trans. W. F. Trotter (New York: Random House, 1941), 74.

p. 95 Richard J. Foster, Dallas Willard, Walter Brueggemann, and Eugene H. Peterson, eds., *The Life with God Bible* (San Francisco: Harper-One, 2005), 530.

p. 96 Dallas Willard, *The Spirit of the Disciplines: Understanding How God Changes Lives* (San Francisco: HarperOne, 1988), 163.

p. 103 I was interested to read in Susan Cain's remarkable book, *Quiet*, how many other introverts also hate small talk. I highly recommend *Quiet* to anyone looking for insight about how introverts (and extroverts, for that matter) view the world.

7. Worship

p. 109 Epigraph: Frederick Buechner, *Beyond Words: Daily Readings in the ABC's of Faith* (San Francisco: HarperOne, 2004), 414–15.

p. 110 *The Life with God Bible* defines worship as: "expressing in words, music, rituals, and silent adoration the greatness, beauty, and goodness of God, by means of which we enter the supranatural reality of the *shekinah*, or glory, of God." Richard J. Foster, Dallas Willard, Walter Brueggemann, and Eugene H. Peterson, eds., *The Life with God Bible* (San Francisco: HarperOne, 2005), 534.

p. 113 Evelyn Underhill, *Worship* (Eugene, OR: Wipf and Stock, 1989), 4.

p. 115 Henri J. M. Nouwen, *Our Greatest Gift: A Meditation on Dying and Caring* (San Francisco: HarperOne, 1994), 23–24.

p. 117 Exodus 15.

p. 117 1 Samuel 18:10.

p. 117 1 Chronicles 25:1.

p. 117 Psalm 96:1.

p. 117 Eugene H. Peterson, *A Long Obedience in the Same Direction: Discipleship in an Instant Society* (Downers Grove, IL: InterVarsity Press, 2000), 54.

8. Failure and Fasting

p. 124 Timothy F. Simpson, footnotes to 2 Samuel 12:16, in Richard J. Foster, Dallas Willard, Walter Brueggemann, and Eugene H. Peterson, eds., *The Life with God Bible* (San Francisco: HarperOne, 2005), 462.

p. 125 Luke 4:2b.

p. 134 Kathleen Norris, *The Quotidian Mysteries: Laundry, Liturgy, and "Women's Work"* (New York: Penguin, 1998), 15.

9. Service

p. 139 Epigraph: Richard J. Foster, *Celebration of Discipline*, rev. ed. (San Francisco: HarperOne, 1998), 126.

p. 143 Thomas R. Kelly, *A Testament of Devotion* (San Francisco, HarperOne, 1941), 99–100.

10. Celebration

p. 153 Epigraph: Dallas Willard, *The Spirit of the Disciplines: Understanding How God Changes Lives* (San Francisco: HarperOne, 1988), 181.

p. 153 John 15:11.

p. 153 Willard, *Spirit of the Disciplines*, 179.

p. 158 G. K. Chesterton, *Orthodoxy* (San Francisco: Ignatius Press, 1908), 165.

p. 159 Ibid., 167.

p. 163 Matthew 2:10.

p. 164 Richard J. Foster, *Celebration of Discipline*, rev. ed. (San Francisco: HarperOne, 1998), 193.

Conclusion: Grace and More Grace

p. 169 Thomas R. Kelly, *A Testament of Devotion* (San Francisco: HarperOne, 1998), 97.

p. 170 Martin Luther, "The Estate of Marriage," Part III, 1522, available online at http://pages.uoregon.edu/dluebke/Reformations441/LutherMarriage.htm.

Julia Roller is an author and editor. Her books include *A Year with God* (with Richard J. Foster), *A Year with Aslan*, and *25 Books Every Christian Should Read*. Working with Renovaré, she has also co-authored four spiritual formation guides, including *Connecting with God*, *Learning from Jesus*, *Living the Mission*, and *Prayer and Worship*. She has written study guides for authors such as Desmond Tutu, Richard J. Foster, Henri Nouwen, Jenna Bush, and Rob Bell. Her articles have appeared in the *San Francisco Chronicle*, *Street Spirit*, *Group*, *Rev.!*, and *Children's Ministry*. She and her family live in San Diego, California.